GLORIOUS PRESSED FLOWER PROJECTS

GLORIOUS PRESSED FLOWER PROJECTS

Cellestine Hannemann

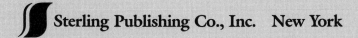

Sterling Publishing Co., Inc.   New York

Edited by Claire Wilson

Library of Congress Cataloging-in-Publication Data

Hannemann, Cellestine.
   Glorious pressed flower projects / by Cellestine Hannemann.
     p.   cm.
   Includes index.
   ISBN 0-8069-7350-1
   1. Pressed flower pictures.   I. Title.
   SB449.3.P7H36   1991
   745.92'8—dc20   90-47828
                                         CIP

10 9 8 7 6 5 4 3 2 1

Published in 1991 by Sterling Publishing Company, Inc.
387 Park Avenue South, New York, N.Y. 10016
© 1991 by Cellestine Hannemann
Distributed in Canada by Sterling Publishing
c/o Canadian Manda Group, P.O. Box 920, Station U
Toronto, Ontario, Canada M8Z 5P9
Distributed in Great Britain and Europe by Cassell PLC
Villiers House, 41/47 Strand, London WC2N 5JE, England
Distributed in Australia by Capricorn Ltd.
P.O. Box 665, Lane Cove, NSW 2066
Manufactured in the United States of America
All rights reserved

Sterling ISBN 0-8069-7350-1

TO
MY HUSBAND, ART, A PATIENT MAN
WHO LEARNED TO COOK

BLACK AND WHITE PHOTOGRAPHS
By Arthur Hannemann

DRAWINGS
By Bonita Hannemann-Reese

COLOR PHOTOGRAPHS
By Adam V. Barnes
Los Angeles, California

Table of Contents

— 1 —
Overview

In one quantum leap, this book takes the art of creating pressed-flower pictures out of the Victorian Age and into the 20th Century, introducing totally new concepts that accommodate the very special needs of each species of flower. These never-fail methods banish forever the shrunken, mouldy, discolored pressed flowers of yesteryear.

In the beginning, it seemed to me to be an unfathomable riddle that so few flowers could be pressed successfully. I soon became more and more determined to work out a solution to this puzzle, so that my dried, pressed flowers would capture the very essence of each flower's natural beauty. When I became better acquainted with the flowers and learned to understand their independent natures, my pressings improved in color and shape. My successful experiments led me to the development of several new techniques: basic press with polyester fibrefill padded pressboards for simple garden flowers, a borax-mattress press for more complex flowers, the use of a microwave oven for flowers that have special needs, and the use of powdered tempera chalk to hasten the drying process.

Types of Presses

PAPER

Paper is a poor medium for pressing flowers because it doesn't press flowers—it smashes them!

Slamming a flower between the pages of a book or the stacks of paper in a conventional press bruises the delicate petals, which causes them to decay and turn brown just as an apple turns brown after it falls to the floor. The thick parts of the flower are crushed between the rigid stack of papers, while the thin petals of the flower, left unsupported by the unyielding paper, shrivel up into strings. Moreover, moisture collects in the thirsty absorbent paper and invites mould. Any moist, bruised vegetation left for more than seven days in a dark, airless enclosure will most assuredly decay.

A flower press should not be used for squeezing moisture out of a flower either. Excessive pressure does not hasten the drying process. It only leads to further bruising of the flower. Without any help from us, the flowers freely shed their moisture through the cut stem where the circulatory system has been interrupted. Only light to moderate pressure is needed against the flowers, such as that provided by polyester fibrefill pads.

THE BASIC PRESS

Polyester-fibrefill-padded pressboards are a much friendlier way to support the back of a blossom. But don't use polyester on the front of the flower. That side gets flattened against a sheet of chipboard. (Chipboard is "raw" cardboard that does not have a slick, shiny finish.) Polyester, neither thirsty nor absorbent, allows moisture to evaporate so that mould is not a threat. Petals will not shrivel or shrink in a polyester-padded pressboard. Its soft springy fibres offer complete support, adjusting to the changing contours of the flower as it is pressed flat. Both thick and thin parts of the flower are held firmly but gently in place without being smashed or bruised. Springs under the press maintain constant gentle pressure

Illus. 1-1. Thick flowers should be pressed in thickly-padded pressboards.

Illus. 1-2. Thin flowers should be pressed in thinly-padded pressboards.

against the flowers. Thick polyester-fibrefill-padded pressboards are used for large, thick flowers and thin padded pressboards are used for small, thin flowers (Illus. 1–1 and 1–2).

THE BORAX MATTRESS PRESS

There is no one-size-fits-all flower press that can be carelessly and indiscriminately applied to any old flower. Each flower has a tolerance level of its own, and, unless the press fits it to a "T," it will stubbornly shrivel up, develop mould, lose all its color, or turn an ugly brown. Flowers, just like people, have personalities of their own—a flower press that suits one flower perfectly can be quite distasteful to another. Yet the two flowers may tolerate other factors in mutual harmony. There are a few flowers that are hardy survivors, retaining color and shape no matter what kind of press is foisted upon them, but the vast majority of flowers are touchy prima donnas who balk at the prospect of entering such unrefined and unsophisticated quarters as a book. Because a flower cannot change its very nature, it is we who must alter our approach to meet the needs of each particular flower.

Bruising is the cause of most brown discoloration in pressed flowers, especially that of chrysanthemums, which bruise most easily and are the most sensitive to pressure. Some flowers tolerate pressure more than others, but chrysanthemums not at all. In a conventional flower press, a book, or even in the basic press with its polyester-padded pressboards, these tender flowers will turn brown. They must be dried carefully with almost no pressure, on a "mattress" filled with borax (Illus. 1–3) and covered with a thick layer of fluffy polyester fibrefill. This press, though developed for chrysanthemums, is also used for other flowers, such as cattleya orchids, phaleonopsis orchids, and rose petals.

THE MICROWAVE OVEN

Bruising is not the cause of discoloration in other flowers, such as cymbidium orchids, which tolerate pressure well. In this case, as the flower dries, oxidation of certain chemicals such as tannins

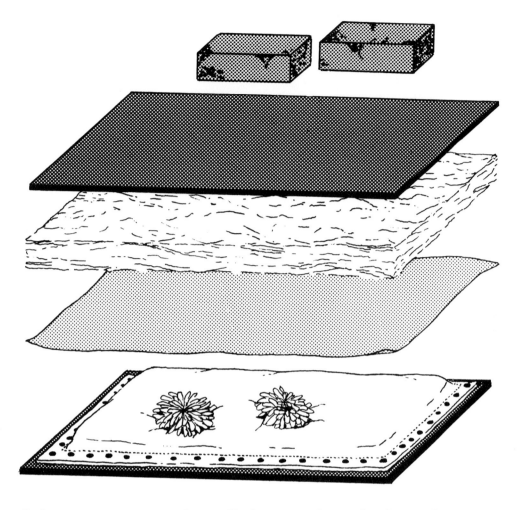

Illus. 1-3. The borax mattress press is indispensable for pressing flowers that do not tolerate pressure well, such as mum daisies.

takes place, causing serious brown discoloration. Microwaves allow obstinate flowers such as these to dehydrate without discoloration. The plant material is prepared in the usual way—the flower is placed on a polyester pad and then a flat sheet of chipboard is pressed against the front of the flower. The brick and pottery weights used to flatten the flowers with the basic and borax mattress press cannot be used in a microwave oven. Marble or glass must be used instead because pockets of air in the bricks and pottery gobble up all the power of the microwaves, leaving the flowers to turn an ugly brown—even in the mi-

crowave. A microwave oven is also handy to use as a quickie method for drying almost any flower that might be needed immediately.

Color

DURABILITY

Heretofore, color has been a major problem in pressed-flower pictures. Very few flowers retain their natural coloring longer than a year. The pigments in most flowers are temporary and perishable, and temporary and perishable will always be the fate of the craft without color correction. One year after pressed flowers are exposed to light their colors undergo certain chemical changes. Depending upon the particular flower involved, the color will either be permanent, semipermanent, faded, bleached away entirely, or turn to a rust red color.

A competent artisan who has tested the color durability of flowers will be able to visualize changes that occur as the flowers age. When choosing flowers for a design, a craftsperson will complement flowers that have durable natural color with hand-colored flowers when needed. His or her expertise in this regard will be evident after the picture has aged.

ADDING COLOR

Adding color in a subtle way will substantially improve a flower's natural durability without adding an artificiality that would be at odds with the charm of a pressed-flower picture. Dry tempera chalk, mixed to match the natural color of the flower and then dusted on the flower before pressing is one of the best methods. The chalk hastens the drying process, prevents discoloration, sets the natural color, and adds color for durability.

Although chalk is the most efficient way to add durability to pastel-colored flowers, bright colors are best treated for lasting effect with felt-pen ink, applied after the flowers have dried.

When durable harmonious color, both natural and treated, is present, a few perishable flowers in the arrangement can add charm, but not disaster. Good design survives both lives—the new and the old.

In some cases, both chalk and felt-pen ink are used—chalk as an aid to drying and felt-pen ink for permanent color. Tiger lilies and daffodils, when dried without the aid of chalk, will sometimes dry a very dull version of the original color. When the petals of these flowers are dusted with powdered tempera chalk, they dry with good, clean, clear color. Though pigments from the chalk absorbed by the petals will add color, the color must be further enhanced with an application of felt-pen ink to match the color of the flower after it has dried. Neither chalk nor ink can be used as a cover-up for petals that have dried with brown discoloration. Discoloration will show through both chalk and ink.

Perspective

If we compare pressed plant materials as a medium for artistic expression to other mediums such as watercolors, acrylics, pastels, or pen-and-ink drawings, we see that each is a unique medium and each has built-in limitations. Watercolorists cannot achieve the same effect as artists working in acrylic, nor can pastel drawings imitate pen-and-ink sketches.

So it is with pressed-flower pictures. The medium has built-in limitations. Unlike the others, however, its potential has never developed beyond the most primitive stages. Along with better methods for pressing flowers and greater color durability, a third stage of improvement is important—perspective.

Perspective is a technique used in two-dimensional media to create an illusion of depth on a flat surface. The stilted, static, lifeless appearance of pressed plant materials can be changed to one of movement, action, and liveliness when the artistry of perspective is added (Illus. 1–4). This can be achieved through proper manipulation of the pressed plant materials. The round center of a daisy or a narcissus can be pressed in such a way as to create an oval shape. This shape in the middle of a flower makes it appear to be facing sideways instead of head on.

The appearance of three dimensions can also be achieved when certain flowers are dismantled and reassembled. For example, whole lilies, orchids, and daffodils, with their five or six petals all shooting off in different directions, are difficult to control in a press. However, when petals of these flowers are dismantled, pressed individually, and then reassembled, an interesting illusion of depth can be added.

Other methods of adding perspective include foreshortening petals, folding leaves, and placing

Illus. 1-4. By pressing these florets of Queen Anne's lace in several views, the artist created an illusion of depth in this otherwise flat design.

flowers between or behind leaves. Nodding flowers, placed at the end of curved stems, create the feeling of the weight and movement of a live flower bending on its fragile stem.

Mounting Pressed-Flower Pictures

The design of a pressed-flower picture is limited only by the imagination, provided the design is allowed to grow and develop in an unrestricted environment, unobstructed by impractical technicalities. Until recently, glue or egg white was universally recommended for mounting the flowers. However, any method that restricts freedom of movement, such as holding flowers in place with glue, impedes the design process. Designing involves a great deal of put-and-take. No sooner is a flower or leaf placed "just so" than the addition of another flower makes it necessary to either shift, remove, or replace the flower. The relationship and positioning of all the flowers and leaves are dependent upon all the other flowers and leaves in the arrangement, so there is a great need for mobility as the design develops. Right up to the last moment, when the arrangement is ready for framing, much shifting, changing, and adjusting of details in the design takes place.

Although glue might not interfere in arrangements with very simple designs, this would not be true of an elaborately detailed design made up of many bits of vegetation from a variety of sources. If an elaborate design was disturbed to apply glue on each tiny wisp of vegetation, the whole arrangement would be knocked out of balance. In a truly well designed arrangement, the placement of each flower, leaf, and bud is critical to the relationship of all the others. This relationship cannot be disturbed without destroying the delicate balance of the design.

Again it is the polyester fibrefill that steps in to improve the workability and the appearance of the finished product. When flowers are mounted against fabric-covered polyester fibrefill, no glue is needed to hold the vegetation in place. Nor will the arrangement be disturbed as it is handled for framing. The pressure applied against the flowers by the glass holds everything in place, making the tiniest wisp of vegetation secure. The springy polyester fibres behind the background fabric push the vegetation firmly against the glass, making glue unnecessary.

Commercial Possibilities

Pressed-flower pictures have enchanted many, from pauper to princess, and some pursue the craft with a passion. At first we are content to let friends and family lovingly display our work in their homes, but sooner or later there comes a yen to go commercial. Sidewalk craft shows and consignment shops can be rewarding, but they are often inconvenient and tenuous outlets. There is a great demand, however, for preserving wedding bouquets as a service to brides, but the market is barely tapped. Many women are extremely sentimental about their wedding bouquets and are eager to have them preserved. If an artisan has perfected his or her skills in the craft, a little advertising brings a good amount of business and will most certainly be followed by an uninterrupted flow of referrals.

You might want to consider preserving wedding bouquets after acquiring a degree of proficiency in pressing, arranging, and framing flowers. It is a service provided during a happy time of your customer's life and can be a pleasant association with the bride, groom, parents, and attendants. The bouquet should be delivered to your door by an attendant the night of the wedding and then picked up by the bride three or four weeks later when it has been completed and framed.

Preparing for arts and crafts fairs, on the other hand, can be grueling work. Thousands of flowers, leaves, vine tendrils, and such must be grown and pressed months in advance. Many flowers, such as larkspurs, pansies, lobelias, and forget-me-nots, are not available at flower shops and must be either grown or acquired from nurseries. You will also need to prepare about twice the merchandise you expect to sell. The public expects a variety of choices in a variety of colors. Building a display, setting it up, and dismantling it each day of the fair all require a lot of work. However, you meet the nicest people! Craftspeople surround you, also selling their wares. The craft-seeking customers are different, too. They are more appreciative of the effort craftspeople give to their work. Often they are looking for something different from the items found in every shop on the avenue. If it is a popular craft show that has been well advertised, thousands of people will pass your display.

This can make for profitable sales of novelty items like pressed-flower crafts. Seldom will a shop having a thousand customers a day take your work on consignment. Another plus for arts and crafts shows is the opportunity for you to experiment with new designs, stretch your creative horizons, and learn from public opinion.

2

Selecting Flowers To Press

A large and varied collection of pressed plant materials is essential when designing pictures. You must collect many flowers and leaves in all sizes, shapes, and colors, as well as gracefully curved stems, grasses, ferns, weeds, and small sprays. Tiny buds and vine tendrils are nice to have on hand for adding delicately detailed embellishments to a design. Collect tiny flowers or florets (Illus. 2–1) to add interesting details to an arrangement. Florets are small flowers that grow close together and form a large flower. Single spirea florets, for example, are dainty little flowers, and their buds are like miniature rose buds with charmingly delicate calyxes. However, most multipetalled flowers do not press well. The crowded layers of petals form indistinguishable blobs after these flowers have been pressed.

Study the various shapes and colors of leaves (Illus. 2–2). Leaves, ferns, and weeds are not as sensitive as flowers and can be pressed in weighted telephone books with good results. An interesting selection and variety of leaves can be just as important as the flowers in an arrangement. When a design seems lacking, try adding leaves of contrasting shape and texture to those already being used in the design. Repetition of leaves can be as uninteresting as that of flowers.

Press leaves separately or in sprays. If rose leaves are picked soon after opening and before the chlorophyll colors their leaves green, they will dry a rich mahogany color. Miniature rose bushes generally bear small leaves, whereas bushes with large flowers develop very large leaves, sometimes unsuitable for pressed flower arrangements. Pointed leaves can be used to advantage—they introduce and/or strengthen the flow of movement, indicating direction and line in an arrangement.

Leaves with silver backs are excellent when placed against a dark background with the silver side up. Some weeds are very decorative (Illus. 2–3) in pressed flower pictures, particularly grass that has gone to seed.

Commercially bleached fern and lacy, skeletonized leaves (Illus. 2–4) are particularly nice for pressed-flower pictures when trimmed to a suitable size. Commercially dyed leaves and brightly colored grasses are excellent for pressed-flower pictures, and their color is permanent.

A few visits to your local nursery will help you identify plants and flowers by name. Seed catalogs or guide books with colored pictures of flowers will familiarize you with varieties that you might want to consider growing for pressing. The alphabetical guide in the back of this book rates a number of flowers for their natural color

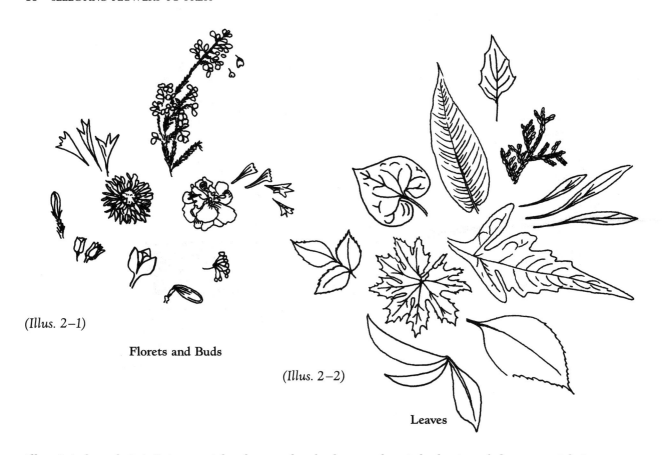

(Illus. 2–1)

Florets and Buds

(Illus. 2–2)

Leaves

Illus. 2-1 through 2-4. It is essential to have on hand a large and varied selection of plant materials in order to create truly unique pressed-flower pictures.

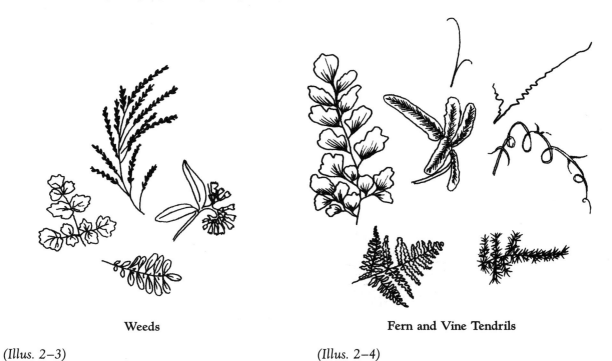

Weeds

Fern and Vine Tendrils

(Illus. 2–3)

(Illus. 2–4)

durability along with suggestions for adding color to them with either dry tempera chalk, before the flower has been dried, or felt-pen ink, after the flower has dried. Flowers not listed there should be tested and the results recorded for future reference.

Many wildflowers (Illus. 2–5) are on the endangered list and many others are on lists of nearly endangered species. In our enthusiasm for collecting flowers to press, we must restrain ourselves where wildflowers are growing. These flowers must depend upon the whims of nature in order for their seeds to germinate. Propagation under natural conditions is often precarious. Out of thousands of seeds, only a few per year might germinate to produce a flower under adverse weather conditions. Because the flowers produce seeds, the survival of a whole species could depend upon the few flowers that we might have picked.

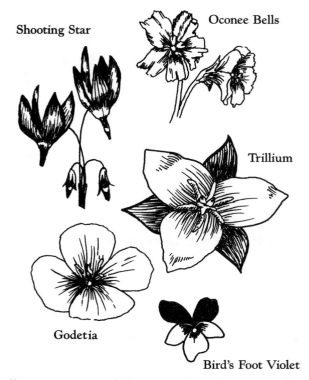

Illus. 2-5. Many wildflowers such as those pictured above, are endangered. Although they might seem perfect for an arrangement, such plant life should be left untouched.

Choosing Flowers To Press

Flowers should be picked in the afternoon when the plant is systemically dry. Do not pick flowers that are wet with dew or that have been soaked by recent rain. If the rainy season continually thwarts your efforts to harvest choice specimens for pressing, you might have better luck if you grow the flowers in pots or in planter boxes. Then you can move them under a roof where moisture can be controlled. In the San Fernando Valley in California, where the growing season is dry, I still favor planter boxes for controlling soil conditions and exposure to the sun. When the sun beats down unmercifully in our minus humidity, with temperatures in the 100s, the flowers begin to fade a few hours after they have opened.

Flowers that have been bruised by animals and by people brushing against them will dry with brown scars. Mud and water spots spattered on the flower will be more visible after the flower has dried than when it was alive and will show up as colorless or brown scars. Flowers picked the day they open will probably not have been subjected to spatters or bruises and will be at their peak of color, whereas three or four days after a flower has opened it will be faded from the sun and much of the color will be gone. Sickly plants produce flowers with faded, poor color even on the day their flowers open.

Single flowers, as opposed to double varieties, are almost always better subjects for pressing. Single varieties of leptospermum, spirea, and geranium are much preferred over the double varieties. Extra petals on double geraniums can be removed to reduce the flower's bulk. Additional layers of petals lengthen the drying time. The longer it takes for a flower to dry, the greater the chance for decay to set in and discolor the flower.

Many flowers that are very deep purple or deep red dry almost black and are not too appealing in a pressed-flower picture. The presence of blue in these flowers causes them to darken because blue is a dominant color in pressed flowers and will have its way wherever it is present.

(There are more blue flowers that can be rated superior for their color durability than any other color in pressed flowers.) White roses and dendrobium orchids that have been pressed while still green—before the flowers have fully matured—dry a pale green color even when white chalk is applied. Therefore, these flowers should be allowed to mature in water before pressing.

Round, trumpet-shaped flowers do not lend themselves well to being pressed. A morning glory, petunia, or hollyhock, when pressed full face, looks like a big shapeless pancake and has little appeal. Pressed on its side in profile, it is a little bit better. I have seen a morning glory, pressed in profile (with its calyx and a bit of stem attached), used in a whimsical design where it was turned upside down and used as the bonnet of a little girl standing in a garden.

Some flowers will begin to wilt soon after they have been picked and must enter the press quickly. Take the flower press along if you are picking flowers from a friend's or neighbor's garden so that there is not a long delay before the flowers enter the press. Flower heads held in your hand wilt faster than those in an airy basket.

Orchids and chrysanthemums, which systemically retain a great deal of moisture, will probably be pressed with better results a few days after they have been picked. However, if these flowers are taken from a wedding bouquet, where they have been out of water all day, they should be pressed without delay.

When pressing a flower, you must also consider the shape and thickness of its calyx and sepals. The calyx is the thick growth at the base of a flower where all of its petals are joined together. The sepals are the green, leaflike bracts attached to the calyx (Illus. 2–6). Daisies and roses have extremely heavy calyxes just below the petals. The calyxes of some trumpet-shaped flowers are located far below the face of the flower. In these cases, the tubular growth immediately below the face of the flower, as well as its calyx, can be trimmed away.

Flowers such as sweet william cannot be trimmed in this manner because each separate petal is joined at the calyx, far below the face of the flower. These flowers must be pressed with the calyx attached.

I prefer to use flowers that have been pressed without their stems for two reasons. First of all, most stems stick straight out and are unattractive. Second, stems retain a great deal of moisture and, during the drying process, can prevent the flower from drying quickly, because the flower seemingly draws moisture from the stem. Some, like sprays of lobelia or forget-me-not, dry very quickly with or without stems, but many flowers do not. A better selection of stems can be had by collecting the gracefully curved stems of whatever source is available—weeds, grass, vines, or flowers. These can be slipped under any flower to follow the lines that are developing in the design. This is better for the design, because if you try to determine the placement of a flower while its stem dangles below, it can influence style and direction and have a limiting effect on the imagination.

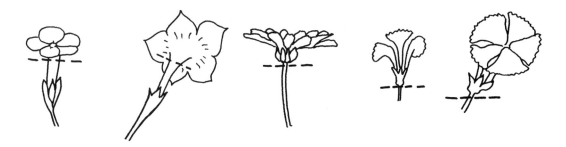

Illus. 2-6. Calyxes and sepals (the parts of a flower that hold the petals together) vary from plant to plant. Some can be kept and pressed, but others are too stiff or thick and must be discarded.

Storing Pressed Flowers

Small amounts of pressed flowers can be stored in plastic bags. With this method of storage, the flowers can be easily seen for selection through the clear plastic. Static electricity will keep the flowers flat during storage.

Pressed flowers can also be stored in boxes lined with tissue paper. This method is more practical when large supplies of the same flower are being stored. In the cover of the box, place a few layers of tissue. On the tissue, lay the flowers close together but not overlapping. Cover the flowers with several layers of tissue, then add another layer of flowers, and so on, ending with a layer of tissue on top.

Finally, treat a sheet of shelf paper with insecticide and lay it on top of the last tissue layer. This will insure against invasion by insects.

Insert the bottom of the box down on top of the shelf paper so that it nests inside the cover (Illus. 2–7).

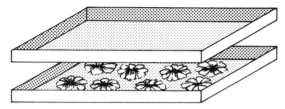

Illus. 2-7. Store leftover pressed flowers between sheets of tissue inside a dry cardboard box.

Then place rubber bands around the box to provide a little pressure against the flowers, which will keep the petals from curling.

Leaves are not as sensitive as flowers, and most can be stored loose in boxes without pressure. A sheet of paper between each layer of leaves will be an aid when selecting leaves from the box. Store pressed flowers and leaves in a dry area up off the floor.

— 3 —
Color

When speaking of a pressed flower's color, we need to know the time frame to which we are referring. Is it the original color of the flower immediately after it has been pressed, the color one year after it has been mounted in a frame and exposed to light, or the color five or ten years down the road? "Does it keep its color?" someone asks. "When?" we might ask in return. The ideal flower is one with properties that allow it to be pressed with retained color, and then to hold that color as it ages. Only a few flowers fall into this category. But with a little help from us, all flowers can be dried with a reasonable facsimile of their live color intact. However, only the addition of color, using chalk or felt-pen ink, can help some flowers to age gracefully.

Natural Color

First, let's examine the natural color of flowers and leaves and the possibilities of color retention one, five, and ten years later. Then we will weigh the pros and cons of adding color to the flowers to improve their durability.

When a flower is initially pressed, the natural color it retains might fall into one of five categories illustrated here, depending on the particular flower involved.

The flower at the top of the diagram (Illus. 3–1) is labelled RED and represents the color of the live flower in this example.

To the left, below the "live" flower, is a second flower, also labelled RED. It represents flowers that dry the exact color of the live flower.

The next flower is labelled BRIGHT RED. This represents salmon-red roses and salmon-colored geraniums (also in the rose family) that dry a bright red. Peach-colored flowers in the rose family dry a pretty pink. The absence of blue pigments in these flowers allows the red pigments to dry a more vivid color. On certain occasions, these color changes will be desirable. At other times, the original color must be stabilized with an application of powdered tempera chalk.

The third flower in the second row is labelled MAROON to represent those flowers that will dry a darker color than the color of the live flower. For example, in this category, a deep red rose will dry a maroon or burgundy color. The blue pigments in this flower will cause the reds to darken as the flower dries.

Blue is a dominant color in pressed flowers. It will have its way wherever it is present, altering pink to lavender, red to maroon, or purple to navy blue. In white delphiniums, there is a faint trace of blue that cannot be seen until the flower has dried and the color changes to gray. However,

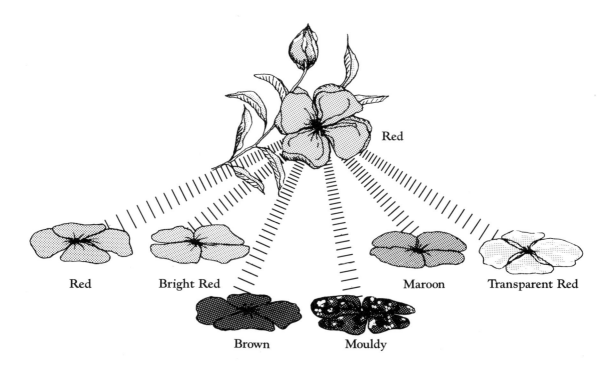

Illus. 3-1. This diagram demonstrates the various color changes that may occur in a flower once it has been dried and pressed. In this example, red was the color of the live flower.

an application of chalk before drying will stabilize the color of white delphiniums. I know of no chemical that will prevent red roses from darkening.

Purple Johnny-jump-ups are also in the maroon category, drying a navy blue color. Though flowers in this category do not retain the exact color of the live flower, they are nevertheless acceptable, as long as they have no brown discolorations.

To the far right is a flower labelled TRANSPARENT RED. This flower represents those flowers that become thin and transparent when dried. Crocuses and moss roses are among these. Though their color might be acceptable, without brown discolorations, the transparent quality of these flowers diminishes the density of color. The color is further diffused when displayed against a contrasting background color. An application of felt-pen ink or chalk can be used to intensify the color.

Below these examples of red color are two others, one labelled BROWN and one labelled MOULDY. They represent flowers that have suffered damage. This often occurs in the press, either from bruising or prolonged confinement. Neither of these results need happen if the correct techniques are used on the flower.

Flowers can also be bruised and damaged even before they enter a press—in the garden. Animals and people may brush against them or mud and water may be spattered on their petals. All will bruise the flowers. Though not visibly prominent on the live flower, bruises reveal themselves as either colorless or brown scars after the flower dries. Pick the flowers on the day they open, before the busy life of the garden has subjected them to bruises and spatters.

FRESHNESS

The color of a flower will be strongest on the day it opens, provided the plant is healthy and thriving. Weak color can sometimes be attributed to sickly plants. A flower that has been on a plant for three days, exposed to sun, sprinkled with rain, or watered a few times will have faded a little each day, and much of the original color will be gone. Again, pick flowers the day they open. If a plant is covered with blossoms, it will be difficult to determine which have opened recently, so nip off all the flowers and discard them. On succeeding days, pick and press the fresh new blooms as they appear.

DRYING TIME

Decay threatens when a flower has taken too long to dry. How long is too long? Enclosing a moist flower more than five days in a dark, airless press invites decay. The flowers must dry before decay has a chance to set in. Some flowers retain a great deal of systemic moisture and will take longer to dry. Heat, chalk, or microwaves accelerate the process. Flowers from plants that have recently been saturated from heavy watering, rain, or dew will also take longer to dry. These blooms should be avoided when choosing flowers to press.

NATURAL COLOR OF LEAVES

With proper treatment, leaves and fern can be dried a true representation of their original color—green, mahogany, variegated, and white in spring and summer and red and yellow during autumn. Leaves are a much tougher form of growth than petals and do not bruise in any type of press. Most are perfectly happy to be pressed between the pages of a book, but they should be selected carefully and examined for cuts and bruises. Damaged spots on the leaves will become visibly prominent scars after the leaves have dried.

Green leaves generally dry green without any help, but the addition of heat shortens the drying time and sharpens the color to a brighter green. Put the press in the oven with only the pilot for heat. If high heat is applied before of after the leaves have dried, they could become scorched.

Leatherleaf fern or rabbit's-foot fern can be dried satisfactorily with the simple application of heat. However, microwaves should not be used on these ferns. Shrinkage in the microwave oven distorts the proportions of its growth, widening the spaces between leaflets.

Results when pressing asparagus fern with or without heat are very unreliable—sometimes the green is retained, but often the needles turn yellow. Microwaves are more reliable for drying asparagus fern. Results are perfect every time.

Fall leaves retain their interesting colors when dried without heat and very young leaves, such as rose and nandin, that are picked before chlorophyll has colored them green, will dry a rich mahogany color without heat.

White leaves, such as those from the dusty miller plant, dry gray, but white chalk and the addition of heat hastens drying and preserves the white color.

Variegated leaves, such as dieffenbachia, maranta, or Chinese evergreen, retain their interesting colored patterns only when dried in a microwave. If dried any other way, these leaves will consistently turn brown.

Dappled ivy leaves, such as white and green, must be dried in the microwave oven to retain the white areas. If they seem obstinate even in the microwave, use white chalk.

DURABILITY OF COLOR IN FLOWERS

One year after a flower has been displayed in a pressed-flower picture you will see changes begin to take place, as demonstrated in the following diagram (Illus. 3–2).

The flower at the top of the diagram is labelled RED and represents the original color of the pressed flower.

Below on the left is a flower also labelled RED, representing those flowers that have aged one year without noticeably fading. Though a certain sharpness of color might be gone, this change is not noticeable unless a newly pressed flower is held up for comparison.

Next in line is a flower labelled PALE RED, which represents those flowers that have faded after one year but have retained some color in their petals.

The third flower is labelled BLEACHED, representing flowers that have lost all their color after they have aged one year. No color remains.

The fourth flower, labelled RUST RED, represents flowers that not only have lost all their color completely after one year, but have turned a rust red color. I have never found a chemical or technique to prevent these flowers from turning rust red. Neither chalk nor felt-pen ink covers this discoloration. The dark color shows right through the coloring agent. There are not many flowers in this category, but all of the succulent blossoms seem to turn rust red after one year.

DURABILITY OF COLOR IN LEAVES

Leaves will begin to change color after one year's exposure to light, and this color change must be reckoned with in the planning stages of a pressed-flower picture. Maidenhair fern is particularly tempting to use as a dominant force in an arrangement, because it dries in wonderfully graceful shapes with brilliant emerald green leaves and jet black stems and spores. Unfortunately, maidenhair fern leaves bleach to white, but the black color of the stems and spores remains.

A few leaves retain their original pressed color for two years but most turn to beige and sepia tones. There is a great deal of variety in the tone of aged leaves. Ivory, rust red, peach, yellow-beige, brown-beige, or near white, depending upon the particular leaf involved. Ivy ages to an ivory color and pine ages to rust red.

Many autumn leaves retain their rich coloring for several years, but not all do. Like flowers, each specific leaf type must be tested for two months on a sunny window ledge to determine its durability. Most young leaves that dry a mahogany color appear to be durable over a period of a few years. The back side of the cotoneaster leaf loses a little of its sharpness, yellowing a bit with age. Dusty miller leaves that have been treated with white chalk retain their color indefinitely. The gray leaves of the acacia hold their color indefinitely, although I find them to be very coarse and woody. When thin delicate flower petals are arranged on top of the woody stems of these leaves, the petals become disfigured with age.

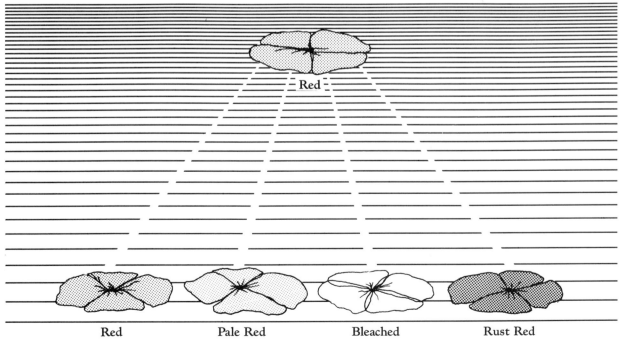

Red

Red   Pale Red   Bleached   Rust Red

Illus. 3-2. The chart above displays the changes that may occur in a flower of a particular color one year after it was pressed.

Variegated leaves such as maranta, dieffen-bachia, and Chinese evergreen age to beige tones, and after a few years their interesting and color-ful patterns are barely distinguishable.

Aging and Care of Pressed-Flower Pictures

On the back of each picture that you sell com-mercially or give as a gift, these instructions should appear: "Do not display in direct sun or under fluorescent lights. Avoid excessively hu-mid locations. The flowers and leaves, once living things, will by their very nature and chemical make-up, eventually fade. Fading varies from flower to flower and may begin anywhere from one to ten years after completion. Leaves will begin to lose their green coloring in a year and will gradually turn to soft beige or sepia tones."

FLUORESCENT LIGHTS AND DIRECT SUN

Fluorescent lights and sunlight can cause dried flowers to fade six times faster than incandescent lights can. Shops always use fluorescent lights because they are cool and economical, so be wary of displaying pictures there. If one of your pressed-flower pictures has been displayed in a shop for six months under fluorescent lights or in the shop window, it will have aged not six months, but three years! An incandescent light placed over a display will protect the flowers by deflecting the path of the fluorescent rays. The thick, translucent plastic covers found on some fluorescent light fixtures also offer some protec-tion against fading. When my flowers were in a gallery, I had an incandescent light set above the display to protect them from the fluorescent ceil-ing lights.

PERISHABILITY

In some flowers, the veins discolor and darken at a more advanced rate than the rest of the petals. This often reveals a network of intricate, beauti-ful patterns weaving their way through the flower, a quality that is not apparent in a freshly dried flower. This kind of change can make the picture more interesting than when it was freshly mounted. Most of the changes in pressed-flower colors occur after the first year's exposure to light. Changes continue with further aging, but at a much slower rate. Depending upon the spe-cific flower and color, dramatic changes will again occur after five years, when many flowers will begin to acquire beige or sepia tones. The color in only a few flowers will hold up for ten years.

Nothing you might do to a flower or leaf will alter the perishable nature of its color. A yellow viola will always lose its color one year after ex-posure to light. A dark blue (but not a light blue) delphinium will retain its color for five years. It doesn't matter if you leave the flower in the press for a longer period of time, apply more or less heat to it, microwave it, apply more or less pressure to it, use polyester padding, or say magic incanta-tions. Nothing will alter the nature of the flower's color as time marches on. The only case in which flowers do appear to hold their color is when they have been embedded in acrylic for use as paper-weights. This is probably due to the total absence of air within the embedment.

Neither can any generalization be made about the durability of certain colors. Though there are more blue flowers with durable color, we cannot say that all blue flowers are durable. Nor can we say that if a flower is yellow, it will lose all of its color at the end of a year even though many do.

When speaking of a specific flower in a specific color, the aging process is predictable and consis-tent, but this does not necessarily carry over to any other flower, even when they are both in the same family. For example, the color of a dark blue larkspur seems permanent, whereas light blue and light pink larkspurs lose their color one year after exposure to light. Durability in each flower is unique to that flower.

TESTING COLOR DURABILITY

In the alphabetic guide at the back of the book, color in various flowers is graded for durability. A simple test will determine the color durability of a flower not listed. Leave the flower on a south-facing windowsill (Illus. 3–3) for two months in the summer, when days are long and the sun shines every day. The flower will then fade, bleach, and age the equivalent of one year's normal exposure to light. Results will not be accurate if tests are made during the short, cloudy days of winter. Records of results should be kept for future reference and should list the name of the flower, its color, test dates, and a notation to indicate whether the color bleached away altogether, turned to rust, faded just a little, faded a lot, or hardly faded at all.

Newcomers to the craft might find it difficult to believe that a newly pressed flower exhibiting richly vivid colors could fade away to nothing so quickly. By way of explanation, pressed-flower colors might be compared to the perishable dyes of yesteryear when parlor shades had to be drawn if upholstery and draperies were to be protected from fading. So also does a pressed-flower picture need protection, and therefore, should not be hung where the sun shines directly on the glass. Most flowers that are displayed in a constantly darkened room will hold their color much longer than flowers displayed in a room with a bright sunny exposure. However, some flowers have such fragile color that all of it will fade within a year, even if the flower is closed up in a storage box.

Artificial Color

Pressed-flower pictures have been known to lead a double life—here today and gone sour tomorrow (Illus. 3-3). Picture an arrangement that includes vivid orange California poppies, bright purple flowers from the Brazilian glory-bush, the soft blue and yellow of violas, and the sharp green contrast of maidenhair fern. Striking colors? For now, yes. But after one year's exposure to light, all the color in these flowers and in the fern

Illus. 3-3. On the left are a chrysanthemum and a cymbidium orchid that were pressed according to traditional methods. On the right are the same types of flower except that the orchid was chalked and pressed in a microwave oven and the chrysanthemum was chalked and pressed in a borax mattress press.

will be gone. This loss of color is predictable and consistent in these plants because their pigmentation is extremely perishable.

On the other hand, dark blue larkspur, purple wild radish, and red pomegranate flowers will retain their natural color for many years. As stated earlier, the color in some flowers is almost permanent, whereas in others it will fade a little or almost completely. In still others, the color bleaches away entirely. A few flowers turn a rusty red color after one year. Most leaves age to beige and sepia tones after the first year, but gray acacia leaves and white dusty miller leaves will show very little change in color.

Inattention to these variables in pressed-flower colors detracts from the value of a picture. Though flowers with durable natural color are not found in every species, the bright colors of felt-pen ink and the pastel pigments of powdered chalk (Illus. 3–4) can be used to improve durability of these colors, thus expanding the choice of flowers we can use in our designs. Any flower known to be perishable should be colored with felt-pen ink or chalk to match or change the original color. When durability is assured, intricate designs that might require forty hours of effort would then be worth the time spent.

The addition of color is not a substitute used to cover defects. It can only be used on clean flowers that have successfully retained original color. For this reason both chalk and ink are sometimes used, chalk before the flower is pressed to hasten drying and retain color and brightly colored ink after the flower has dried to improve its durability.

FELT-PEN INK

Broad-tipped felt pens are very useful for coloring flowers. Ink should be carefully dabbed onto the petals with very light, gentle strokes to avoid tearing them. Because the dye will be absorbed and will quickly spread through the petals of the flower, the entire flower must of necessity be dyed the same color. It is impossible to dye only one part of a flower. The entire surface of a yellow and brown pansy can be dyed yellow without affecting the brown, but blue pansies with

yellow markings present a problem. Yellow ink spreading into the blue areas will create a green flower, giving it an unnatural appearance.

Broad-tipped felt pens in primary colors are readily available at stationery stores, and full-service art supply stores carry felt pens of every imaginable hue. Unfortunately, felt-pen ink in pale, delicate colors does not always shade the flowers in the way that deep colors do. White flowers from the evergreen pear tree (and perhaps other flowers not familiar to me) are an exception. These flowers absorb the lighter shades of ink quite successfully. Before buying pens in light colors, test the colors on the flowers. Some pens can be dipped in fingernail polish remover to increase the flow of ink or to revive a dry pen.

Some felt pens, generally packaged for school children, lack acetone or alcohol as an ingredient and are not absorbed by the flowers. They simply bead up on the surface of the petals.

Cans of ink for refilling felt pens are available in primary colors where architect's supplies are sold. Although these would certainly be handy for brushing color on the flowers, the ink I purchased did not hold up well in storage. After a few months, it curdled in the can and the mixture separated.

Although felt pens are labelled "permanent," this is only true when the ink is not exposed to full sun. Flowers colored with felt-pen ink will bleach completely if they are displayed in direct sun for 10–12 hours.

Neither vegetable dyes nor watercolors are effective for coloring pressed flowers. They merely bead up on the petals of the flower and are not absorbed.

CRUSHED CHALK OR POWDERED TEMPERA

Light, pastel-colored flowers are best enhanced with an application of chalk (Illus. 3-4). The chalk is applied to the live flower before it is dried. When dry powdered chalk is applied to a flower, it not only accelerates the drying process, but also fixes the natural color of a flower. The chalk, used in combination with heat, dries the

Illus. 3-4. Flowers retain their color much better if they are dusted with either white chalk or chalk that has been mixed to match their color.

flower swiftly, before decay has a chance to set in, and the pigments in the chalk color the petals of the flower, adding durability. Excess chalk must be brushed off later to prevent a tell-tale smear from appearing on the background fabric.

Chalk is a clay product to which color has been added. It is sold in several forms at full-service art supply stores or stores that sell supplies for schools. Dry tempera chalk, meant to be used with water for poster paint, is already powdered and is the most convenient form of chalk to use for dusting the flowers.

Various companies manufacture dry powdered tempera, which is usually sold in one-pound cans. Some of the pigments used in dry tempera colors are not suitable for pressed flowers because the bright color is not evident until water is added. For example, red tempera in its dry form has a very dull color and will not color a bright red carnation. For bright red, either artist's pastels or red lecturer's chalk can be scraped, crushed, and sifted for use on the flowers. In purple, there are some companies that do produce a vivid color in a dry form, but other brands appear to be a colorless gray until water is added.

Lecturers' chalk is a soft, square stick that is easily crushed and comes in a few bright, vivid colors.

Artist pastels, though hard and difficult to crush, have the advantage of being available in some of the colors that are difficult to mix from scratch. A stick of gray or brown pastel is useful to keep on hand for shading white cattleya orchids to add depth and perspective.

Round sticks of chalk made for use on school blackboards are not recommended because they are hard, difficult to crush, and made in unsuitably pale colors.

A selection of dry tempera colors to have on hand for pressing flowers should include white, yellow, orange, violet, dull red, bright red, magenta, and purple. Though the dull red is not bright enough for coloring vivid red carnations, it is useful for mixing shades of pink.

Before dusting the flowers with chalk, the colors must be mixed and blended to match the flowers. Sift the chalk before mixing colors together and crush to a powder any granules that may have formed in the dry tempera.

Start by pouring some white or light-color chalk in a roomy bowl. Add the other colors a little at a time, crushing the chalk with the back of a spoon to thoroughly blend the colors together.

Dab a bit of the chalk on the petals from time to time. If the flower exhibits more yellow than the chalk mixture does, add yellow. If the flower seems more pink—add red or magenta. Mix an extra quantity of each blend and store colors in tightly covered jars for future use.

Following are a few suggested blends:

Pink: white and dull red/white and magenta/ white, dull red, and orange.
Peach: white and orange.
Lavender: white and violet/white and purple/ white, violet, and bright red.
Tangerine: white, yellow, and orange.

For flowers that exhibit two or three colors, a substitute of cornstarch or potter's dry clay can be used. Powdered clay is sold in art supply stores for use in pottery making. The starch or clay will fix the color and hasten the drying process. Flowers treated with cornstarch or powdered clay retain their original color and markings very well but do not enjoy the benefit of added color for durability. The natural color of these flowers may fade or bleach away at the end of a year.

Cornstarch leaves a white residue on the dried flower and clay leaves a gray residue. These can be removed with alcohol or acetone (fingernail polish remover) after the flower has dried. Because starch will cook onto the moist flowers, it cannot be used on a flower dried in a microwave oven.

To apply chalk to live flowers, drop them in a covered bowl with a few tablespoons of chalk mixed to match the flowers (Illus. 3–6). Shake the covered bowl to distribute chalk on the flowers. With tweezers, remove the flowers from the bowl and shake off excess chalk. You should not use your fingers to take the flowers out of the chalk if you want to avoid a mess.

Rub the remaining chalk into petals with your fingers. This can get messy, so work with a piece of facial tissue under the flowers. From time to time, roll up and discard the tissue full of excess chalk to keep it from scattering all over the workbench.

Press the flowers according to the instructions in the Alphabetic Guide.

After the flowers have dried, brush the excess chalk from them and rub the small amount of chalk still remaining into the flowers' petals.

There may be times when chalk will become caked on the petals of flowers such as the cattleya orchid. It must then be removed and reapplied. Rubbing alcohol or acetone brushed on the surface of the petals will dissolve the chalk and remove the pigment from the petals. They can then be wiped off with facial tissue, blotted dry, and then receive a new application of chalk.

To purists who may be offended by the use of a coloring agent, I would advise using colored chalk, which can be removed after the flower has dried. Many flowers dry with very dull colors when unaided by chalk. After the chalk has accelerated the drying process and stabilized the color, it can be removed with alcohol or acetone, leaving the flower in its pristine state.

To apply chalk to a dried flower, brush a small amount of chalk on the flower and rub the chalk into the petals to blend in the pigments. It may sometimes be necessary to add chalk to a flower after it has dried if it has not absorbed pigment well.

To add a blush of pink color around the edges of a white flower or yellow to the throat of a white orchid, or to shade the base of a flower's petals to add depth, rub the second color into the petal after the flower has dried.

COMMERCIAL DYES

Florists use liquid dyes to color carnations. The color is absorbed through the stem and on up into the petals, following the pattern of the flower's veins. Such flowers seem to retain this artificial color indefinitely and only need to be dusted with cornstarch to hasten dehydration.

PAINT

For commercial purposes, when preserving wedding bouquets, stephanotis and gardenia blossoms can be whitened with paint, though this practice is not recommended under any other circumstances. When paint is applied to the surface of a pressed flower, its petals, its shading of color, and its venation will be obliterated. Painted flowers do not show signs of change as they age, introducing an artificiality that is at odds with

SUPPLIES FOR SETTING AND ADDING COLOR
Illus. 3–5. At top left are cornstarch and powdered tempera chalk, the former used to dry multicolor flowers and the latter to dry flowers of one color. The sifter and spoon are useful when separating out and crushing coarse granules in the chalk. The bowl and cover are used to hold the chalk and flower, so you can shake the bowl to distribute the pigment onto the petals. The facial tissues are handy for keeping your work area free from chalk dust. The wax paper is used underneath gardenias and stephanotis to increase workability when painting these blossoms. Tweezers are used to handle the flowers during the arranging process. Brushes and cotton swabs are used to apply paint and chalk to petals. Broad-tipped felt pens can add bright color to flowers whose natural color is perishable. A stick of bright red lecturer's chalk can enhance the natural color of red flowers and gray chalk can be used, with the cotton-tipped swap, to add shading to white flowers. Alcohol is used when making the paint mixture and acetone will dissolve and remove excess chalk from petals. Acetone will also revive dried-out felt pens.

the natural quality of pressed flowers. When choices are possible in artistic designs, use natural flowers that retain their color or add the more acceptable coloring agents of felt-pen ink or chalk. Paint is opaque, but felt-pen ink and chalk are absorbed by the flower and do not impair the visibility of the petals. A subtle change in shading is a charming quality of the natural aging process of pressed flowers.

When preserving wedding bouquets, the stephanotis and gardenias, both sharp white flowers, will often be received in poor condition. Often, the stephanotis may have already begun to dry up and discolor. The pliability of the flowers can be revived if they are placed in a plastic bag to which a dab of water has been added and left overnight in a refrigerator. The next day, the flowers can be straightened to prepare for the press. However, the color cannot be revived and such flowers will dry the color of toast. Although paint seems the most acceptable answer to this problem, it does become a trap, because it is important that your work be consistent. The stephanotis in some bouquets might be in just-picked condition and dry a very acceptable off-white color, but once you have painted stephanotis for one bride, paint you must for the next. Many of your clients will be friends or relatives of those you have served before, and comparisons will be made. Unpainted stephanotis age to toast color and unpainted gardenias age to an uneven gray.

Paint Recipe: The recipe below is for a very small amount of durable paint, enough for one gardenia. For a larger quantity of paint, simply double, triple, or quadruple the basic recipe. Your paint should hold up well when stored in a tightly capped jar and kept in a cool, dark place.

   2 teaspoons of white, dry, powdered tempera, sifted. (I find Driad™ brand best for this application.)
   ½ teaspoon water
   ¼ teaspoon of rubbing alcohol or methyl alcohol.

Add water to the dry tempera, stir to a smooth paste, and then add the alcohol. When humidity is low, more liquid will be needed. Add liquids slowly until the paint reaches the proper consistency—thick enough to cover the flower with one coat, but not so thick that brush marks are difficult to cover.

Be careful to keep the formula balanced. Excessive amounts of alcohol will curdle the mixture. If the paint thickens in storage, thin it by adding alcohol or water a little bit at a time.

Use a soft artist's paintbrush that is about ½" wide. Either natural or nylon bristles can be used, provided they are not blunt and stiff. Such bristles leave heavy brush marks on the flowers.

Brush some of the paint onto a piece of wax paper and then lay the flower on the painted surface, right side up. The flower will adhere to the painted surface, preventing it from curling up or moving about while paint is being applied. Lightly brush one coat of paint onto the flower, removing brush marks by applying gentle strokes in the opposite direction. A dry brush passed lightly over the paint when it has partially dried is also an effective means of removing brush marks. Do not apply a second coat.

If the paint does not adhere well to the flower petals, prime the surface of the flower by removing the first application of paint with heavy pressure, which forces the paint into the pores of the flower's petals. Then apply a new coat of paint immediately after the petal has been primed.

Let the painted flowers dry on the paper for no more than ten minutes. Peel them off the wax paper and lay them on a sheet of plain chipboard that has been padded with two facial tissues. Then cover them with a second piece of chipboard. Do not use fibrefill-padded pressboard at this point because it will cause the painted gardenias and stephanotis to develop ruffled edges. Apply pressure with a brick or with the basic press until dry.

4
Pressing Methods

There are several methods of applying pressure to flowers after they have been placed in the padded pressboards. The simplest employ easily obtained sources of pressure, such as heavy objects or straps that compress the boards. These techniques are best used for sturdy flowers or for short-term storage. The most effective way to press and dry flowers that I have found is to place them in either the basic or borax mattress press or to dry them in a microwave oven. These techniques are explained in great detail below.

Bricks

Illus. 4-1. Pressboards with bricks for pressure.

Bricks can be used to weigh down the padded pressboards. A piece of wood placed on top of the stack but underneath the bricks will add stability. Don't pile the stacks too high, because they may topple over, spilling out all your flowers.

Straps

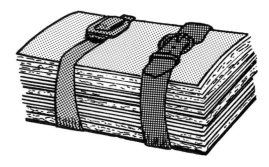

Illus. 4-2. Pressboards with straps for pressure.

Two belts with buckles can also be used to apply pressure. First, place a piece of wood on top of the stack of flowers and another piece under it. Then strap the belts around the stack. The belts must be adjusted every day because pressure will be lost as the flowers begin to change shape and flatten.

Temporary Pressure

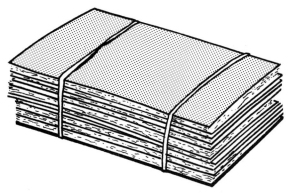

Illus. 4-3. Pressboards with rubber bands for pressure.

When gathering specimens away from home, travelling light is important. In this case, heavy rubber bands can be placed around the padded pressboards in order to hold the flowers for an hour or two.

The Basic Press

The most effective results can be achieved by using the polyester fibrefill-padded basic press. You can either order and assemble a ready-made press or construct one yourself with a few simple parts and tools.

First, you will need three pieces of wood (Illus. 4–4) for the press: one for the cover, another for the platform underneath the flowers, and a third for the base. The size of the press (5½ × 8½) is determined by the size of the padded pressboards. These dimensions should not be enlarged or reduced. Certain flowers, placed in the middle

of a large pressboard, could turn brown because moisture would be trapped in the middle of the press and would not evaporate. This moisture would cause decay and discoloration in the flowers.

BUILDING THE BASIC PRESS

Cover (Illus. 4–5): Cut one piece of ¼" plywood to measure 6½ × 8½ and cut a ⅜" notch in each corner of the cover as shown.
Platform: Cut one piece of ¼' plywood to measure 5½" × 8½".
Base (Illus. 4–6): Cut one piece of ½" plywood to measure 7½" × 8½" and drill a ¼" hole in each corner of the base as shown. These holes should align with the notches in the cover.

Sand the flat surfaces and the edges of the wood with fine sandpaper and remove the dust with a tack cloth. You may then cover the boards with either varnish or paint. You may also decorate the cover with pressed flowers.
Hardware required for the press:

Six coil springs that can be compressed when a
　2½ pound weight is applied
Four ¼" carriage bolts 5½" long, fully threaded
Four jam nuts to fit the bolts
Four wing nuts to fit the bolts
Four washers ⅞" in diameter with a ⅜" hole

Assembling the press (Illus. 4–7):
Staple the six springs to the base of the press, evenly distributing them across the area between the four holes.

The springs will be used to maintain pressure against the flowers as they dry, preventing them from shrinking.

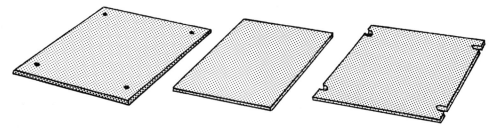

Illus. 4-4. The base, platform, and cover for the basic press, all of which are cut from plywood.

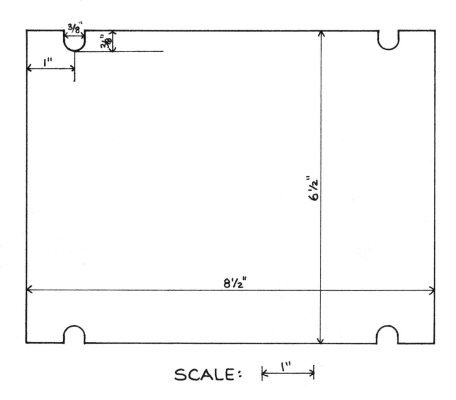

Illus. 4-5 and 4-6. The dimensions for the cover (top) and base (bottom) of the basic press.

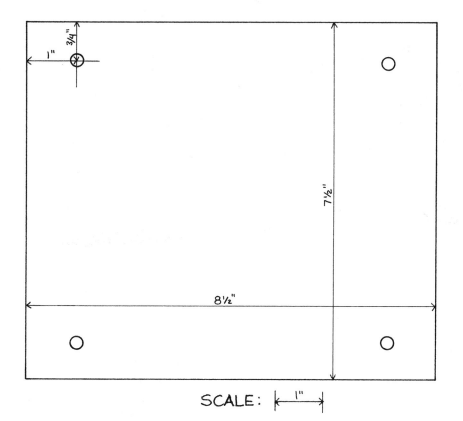

The four carriage bolts are placed in each corner of the press. The four wing nuts are screwed down on the bolts to apply pressure against the stacks of flowers.

To install them, turn the base of the press upside down and insert a bolt all the way through one of the holes. Continue to hold the base upside down and rest the edge of the wood on a hard cement surface, such as a stair. Strike the head of the bolt very firmly with a hammer until it becomes embedded in the round hole.

Turn the base right side up and fasten one of the jam nuts on the bolt until it rests against the base, holding the bolt firmly in place.

Repeat the same procedure until all the bolts and jam nuts are in place.

Assemble all the parts of the press as shown in Illus. 4–8.

Illus. 4-8. The basic press in its completed and filled form.

MAKING PADDED PRESSBOARDS

Two sizes of padded pressboards—1½″ thick and ¼″ thick—are required for pressing flowers in

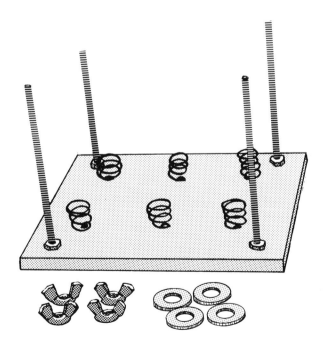

Illus. 4-7. The positioning of the hardware for the basic press. The springs are used to exert pressure against the pressboards filled with plant materials.

the basic press. In order to make the pads, you will glue layers of polyester fibrefill onto pieces of chipboard (unfinished cardboard without a slick, shiny surface) and cover them with nylon or Quiana™ tricot-knit fabric.

Polyester fibrefill is sold in full-service fabric stores. It is available in thicknesses varying from ⅛ of an inch to 3 inches. The quality of the fibres varies considerably. Some are so heavily sized (sizing is a starch-like substance added to the fibres) that they are as stiff and coarse as wire. Others have small fibres tightly compressed into a felt-like fabric. Neither of these is appropriate for pressing flowers. For the pressboards, the padding should be soft, with just enough sizing added to keep its shape.

Instructions are given for assembling 12 thick pads and 12 thin pads. Pads measuring 5½″ × 8½″ give the best results. A pressing surface any larger than this could lead to discoloration of the flowers.

Materials:

½ yard of soft polyester fibrefill around 1¼″ to 1½″ thick, cut into 12 pieces, each measuring 5½″ × 8½″

½ yard soft polyester fibrefill around ¼″ to ½″

Illus. 4-9. A piece of knit fabric, glued on top of the polyester padding will prevent the flowers from becoming tangled in the polyester fibres.

thick, cut into 12 pieces, each measuring 5½″ × 8½″

One yard Quiana™ or nylon tricot-knit fabric (must be a thin, lightweight knit, not woven, fabric) cut into 24 pieces that each measure 5½″ × 8½″.

48 pieces of 5½″ × 8½″ chipboard.

Fabric glue—preferably in a spray can. *Caution:* Only use glue meant for fabrics. Other glues might harden when dry. A proper fabric glue should be soft after drying.

Spray glue over the surface of one sheet of chipboard.

Lay one piece of polyester fibrefill on top of the glued surface.

Gently press down on the polyester pad so that it adheres to the chipboard.

Spray glue over the surface of the polyester fibrefill.

Lay one piece of fabric on top of the glued surface.

Gently press down on the completed pad so the knit fabric sticks to the polyester fibrefill (Illus. 4-9).

Continue gluing pads and fabric on 24 sheets of chipboard until the 12 thick pads and 12 thin pads have been completed.

The remaining 24 pieces of chipboard will be companions to the 24 pads.

USING THE PADDED PRESSBOARDS

Two weights of padded pressboards are used in the basic press. For best results, use a pressboard appropriate to the weight and thickness of the flower to be pressed. Use thin pads (Illus. 4–10) for lightweight, thin flowers and plant parts, such as phlox, violas, alyssum, primroses, forget-me-nots, verbena florets, or geranium florets.

Use thick pads (Illus. 4–11) for heavy, thick flowers and plant parts, such as giant zinnias, marguerite daisies, or delphiniums.

Place the flowers face down on a piece of plain chipboard. Space the flowers close together but don't let them overlap. This can cause bruises and creases on the petals of the flowers. Avoid pressing or flattening the flowers with your hands. This is the work of the press.

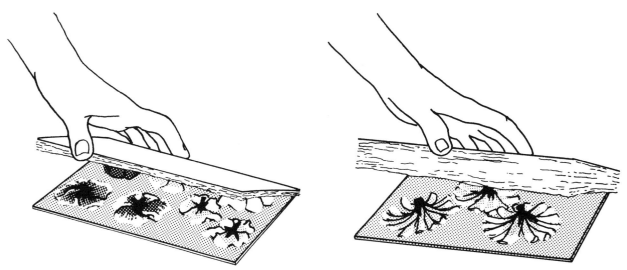

Illus. 4-10 and 4-11. The thick and thin pressboards will increase your success in pressing diverse types of plant materials.

Select the appropriate padded pressboard and place it over the back of the flowers, making a sandwich with the chipboard, flowers, and pressboard.

The polyester pad should always be against the back of the flower and the plain sheet of chipboard against the face of the flower.

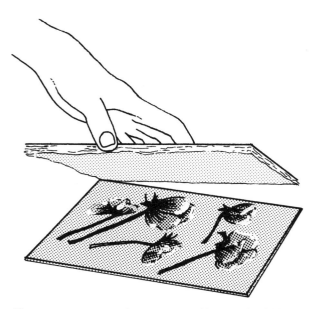

Illus. 4-12. To press flowers in profile, simply fold them in half and lay them on a piece of chipboard. Then press them as you would a full-face flower.

PRESSING FLOWERS IN PROFILE

To press flowers in profile (Illus. 4–12), fold them upwards and lay them on their sides on a plain chipboard sheet. Then cover them with a padded pressboard.

PRESSING BUDS

Press buds and clusters of buds (Illus. 4–13) with their stems attached. Lay them on their sides on plain chipboard and cover them with a padded pressboard.

Buds should be split in two with a knife in order to reduce their moisture content and bulk. Press them with the cut sides against the padded surface.

PRESSING LEAVES, FERN, STEMS, AND VINE TENDRILS

These plant materials are not as sensitive as flowers and do not require special equipment to press well. Telephone books with heavy bricks on top for weight are not only adequate, they also afford a larger pressing area than the pressboards for large sprays of leaves or fern.

Illus. 4-13. In order to press buds successfully, you must first split them in half to reduce the amount of moisture in them.

PRESSING SPRAYS

To press a spray of flowers, which has a stem, leaves, flowers, and buds attached, lay the spray right side up on top of a padded pressboard. Arrange the spray in a graceful line and cover the front of the spray with a piece of chipboard. If the spray is too rigid to arrange, leave it covered for a few hours, then carefully open the pressboard and nudge the spray into the lines you have in mind. After they have become limp, sprays can be coaxed into whatever position you might like, but do not wait too long. After 24 hours in the press the flowers can be difficult to handle and rumple easily. If a stem is unreasonably difficult to coax into position, use a bit of masking tape to hold it in place while it is drying.

PRESSING FLOWERS IN THREE-QUARTER VIEW

Some flowers, such as daisies and narcissi, can be pressed with a small amount of stem attached. When the chipboard sheet is pressed against the flower, the stem will force the flower over on its side a bit and some, but not all, of the flowers, will dry with oval centers.

PRESSING MINIATURE ROSES

These flowers press very well in the basic press, provided the flowers are split in two to reduce their bulk and moisture. Start by slitting the calyx just below the base of the flower (Illus. 4–14). Then cut down through the length of the stem. Next cut upwards through the petals of the flower.

Lay the two halves of the rose (Illus. 4–15) on a chipboard sheet and cover the flowers with an appropriate pressboard. The cut side of the rose should be against the padded surface and the front of the rose should be covered with a plain chipboard sheet.

FILLING THE PRESS

Stack the pressboard sandwiches of flowers on the platform of the press. Then place the cover on top of the stack of flowers.

Push the stack of flowers down with one hand, drop a washer over each bolt, and fasten a wing nut on each bolt (Illus. 4–16).

Continue to push the stack of sandwiches down with one hand while alternately tightening each of the four wing nuts, but only until the

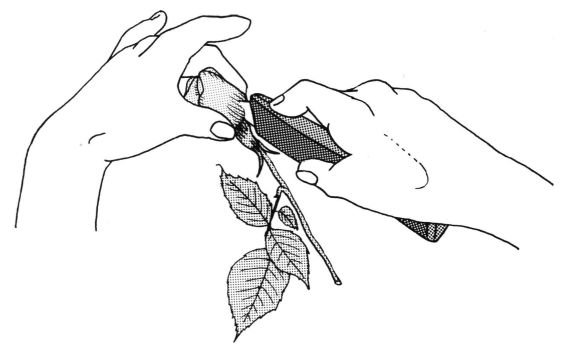

Illus. 4-14. Before you place a rose in the pressboards, you must split it down the middle. Start at the top of the calyx and cut down through the stem. Next, slice up through the petals.

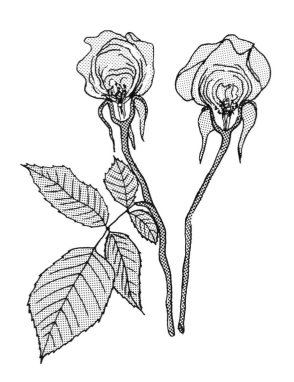

Illus. 4-15. The two halves of the rose should be placed with the cut sides against the plain chipboard and the petals against the padding.

springs at the base of the press have been compressed. Do not continue to tighten the wing nuts once the springs have compressed. Such excessive tightening could cause bruising.

Twenty-four hours after the flowers have entered the press, their rigid calyxes, stems, and buds will begin to wilt, soften, and flatten. At this point you will notice that the springs at the bottom of the press have begun to expand. However, no further adjustments to the wing nuts are necessary while the flowers are drying. Sufficient pressure remains in the springs to prevent shrinkage of the flowers. The springy quality of the polyester fibres will also adjust to the changing shape of the flowers, expanding or compressing to follow the needs of the flowers as they flatten.

DRYING

While the flowers are drying, keep the loaded press in a warm dry place, up off the floor. The flowers dry best in a constant 70° temperature. Avoid areas where there might be wide swings of temperature from 80° in the daytime to 50° at night, such as basements or porches.

Illus. 4-16. The wingnuts on the basic press are used to adjust the pressure against the pressboards.

Do not open the pressboards and disturb the flowers until you are reasonably certain the flowers are dry. After 24 hours the flowers become limp and wilted, about the consistency of wet tissue paper, and will easily rumple if handled. The press can be opened to add more sandwiches of flowers to the stack, provided the sandwiches placed there earlier are not opened.

It is helpful to have the contents of the sandwiches identified. Use rubber bands around each sandwich or batch of sandwiches, and slip a little note under the rubber band that identifies the contents and the date pressed.

How long should the flowers dry? Drying time will vary depending upon the area in which you live, temperature, and humidity. Most small flowers will be dry in four to five days. Verbena florets may dry in as few as two days, whereas pansies may require seven days or longer. I live in an exceptionally hot, dry area, so my own experience with the flowers may not always correspond with the experience of others.

How dry is dry? A dry flower or spray will be stiff and crisp throughout—petals, center, and stem. If the petals appear limp, the flower has probably not dried completely. At first it is helpful to keep notes of the average time needed for drying different kinds of flowers. Flowers that

have not completely dried will sometimes feel cold to the touch. Lay the palm of your hand across the flower. If some parts of the flower feel cold, do not remove the flower from the press. When a flower that is only partly dried is removed from the press, shrinkage and puckering result.

Flowers should always be dried within a maximum of seven days. If humidity is high and the house is cold, the drying process can be hurried along with the application of heat. After working with various flowers for a while, you will be better able to judge when to apply heat.

To apply heat, put the press in a gas oven and use *only the pilot light for heat.* If you don't have a pilot light in your oven, you can preheat it to around 100° and, after *turning off* the burner, put the press in the warm oven. Each day until the flowers are dry, remove the press from the oven, preheat the oven again, turn off the heat, and put the press back in the warm oven. Flowers subjected to high heat will scorch, so it might be wise to tack a little sign to the front of the oven cautioning the family to remove the flowers before using the oven.

REMOVING FLOWERS FROM THE PRESSBOARDS

Most flowers are easy to remove. However, very thin flowers will sometimes adhere to either the chipboard sheet or to the padded surface. To remove these flowers, carefully slip a thin knife blade under the petals to loosen the center of the flower before lifting it. Do not pull on the petals because they may tear.

Flowers picked from plants infested with aphids are sometimes covered with a sticky residue, causing the flowers to stick to the pressboards. These should be avoided when choosing flowers to press.

CARE OF PADDED PRESSBOARDS

Pressboards and chipboards can be used over and over again for many years. To care for padded pressboards, brush off any loose vegetation or chalk clinging to the pads. After the pads have been used five or six times in the basic press, they will flatten out and lose their bounce. Those that have been used in a microwave oven will lose their bounce after only one use and must be revived with steam each time the pads are used. This can be done with steam from a kettle or pot of boiling water (Illus. 4–17) or with a fine mist of water sprayed on the pads, or else the pads can be left outside (protected from rain, of course) on a damp night. However, do not allow the pads to become soaked and make sure that they dry thoroughly before storing them.

Chalk that may have stained the pads will dissipate a bit after the pads have been steamed. Stains that remain on the pads will not interfere with their efficiency or affect the color of flowers pressed in them.

Chipboard sheets can be cleaned with a damp cloth after removing any vegetation stuck to them. To prevent the chipboards from warping after they have been cleaned, stack them in the press to dry.

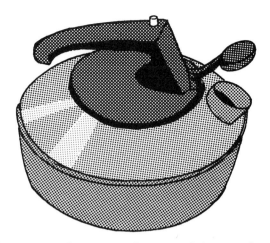

Illus. 4-17. When your polyester pads become flattened with use, you can fluff them up again by holding them over a steaming kettle or pot of water.

ing in a hot dry climate as I do, heat is not often needed to dry flowers in my borax mattress press. However, for homes in humid locations, or in places where winter temperatures drop to 50° and below at night, heat will be needed. The flowers dry best in a constant temperature of 70° or more.

The Borax Mattress Press

Some flowers are too delicate to be pressed in the basic press. These blossoms should instead be dried and flattened on a borax-filled mattress with a covering made of thick polyester fibrefill.

In order to make the mattress (Illus. 4–18), fill a broadcloth fabric bag with borax powder, level it, and tack it down on a piece of tempered Masonite™. Then, depending on the specific flower to be pressed, lay over the flowers a piece of polyester double-knit fabric, a fluffy 4″ blanket of polyester fibrefill, or pieces of both. Cover the stack with a piece of Masonite™, place a suitable number of bricks on top of the press, and store the stack in a dry place.

The press can be built 15″ square, 18″ square, or whatever size you prefer. But, because heat is sometimes necessary when using this press, its size will depend upon the size of your oven. Liv-

Materials

BASE AND COVER OF THE PRESS

Instructions will be given here for a press 18″ square. Either purchase or cut two pieces of ¼″ tempered Masonite (not particle board), each 18″ square. Masonite that is not tempered will not hold tacks well. One piece will serve as the base of the press, the other as the cover.

Cloth bag: Cut two pieces of cotton/polyester-blend broadcloth, each 18¼″ square.

Polyester double-knit fabric: Cut fabric to measure 17″ square. Edges should be left raw. Do not hem.

POLYESTER FIBREFILL BLANKET

For this press, you will need unsized polyester fibrefill, which is sold in full-service fabric stores for quilting. It is packaged in plastic bags in

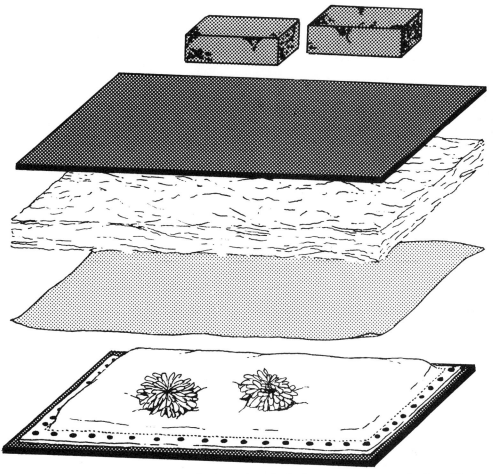

Illus. 4-18. The borax mattress press consists of a base (to which the mattress is attached), a fabric blanket, a thick polyester pad, and a Masonite™ cover. Weight is applied by laying bricks on top of the stack.

amounts large enough to quilt one blanket. The polyester fibrefill used in this press must have absolutely no sizing. Unsized polyester fibrefill is like so many loose hairs that pull apart when casually unwound from a roll. Each layer of batting may be from 1″ to 4″ thick and must be unwound very carefully to prevent the layers from splitting. Manufacturers sometimes insert a thin sheet or narrow strip of paper between layers as an aid to separating them.

Very large rolls of fibrefill can be purchased where professional upholsterers' supplies are sold, but they must always be carefully examined to be sure there is no sizing. A large roll of polyester fibrefill that can stand on end in a fabric store is sized. Unsized polyester fibrefill cannot be made to stand up on end unless the roll has been wrapped in sturdy paper and firmly tied with string.

Cut the polyester fibrefill to make a blanket 17″ square and 4″ high. If the polyester fibrefill is only 1″ thick, you will need to stack several pieces on top of each other.

BORAX

This product is available where laundry products are sold. Do not use silica gel, a desiccant that will absorb moisture from the entire room.

TACKS

Upholstery tacks ¼″ long.

Assembling the Press

Sew together the two squares of broadcloth along three sides and with a narrow seam.

Trim the edges of the seams.

Turn the bag inside out and for added strength stitch to form French seams (Illus. 4–19).

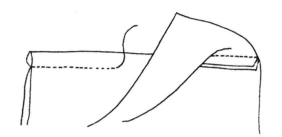

Illus. 4-19. Use French seams to give added strength to the edges of the borax mattress.

Fill the bag with nine pounds of borax. Once the bag is filled, the French seams will protrude around the outside.

Sew the seam on the fourth side of the bag. Then fold it down, sew it, and stitch to make a false French seam.

Lay the bag of borax on top of the Masonite base and flatten it so that the borax is evenly distributed over the surface of the board. The four edges of the bag should be an equal distance from the four edges of the board, so that the bag is evenly centered on the base.

Push a tack through the French seam near each of the four corners of the bag (Illus. 4–20). Tap the tacks down into the board with a hammer. Next, push a tack through the middle of the French seam on each side. Tap the tacks into the board with a hammer while gently stretching the material so that it is taut across the top of the mattress. Finally, insert tacks at 1″ intervals around the remainder of the seams all along the edges of the bag.

Care and Use of the Borax Mattress Press

This press was originally created to press chrysanthemums, but it is also useful for phalaenopsis and cattleya orchids, as well as rose petals. General instructions are given here for the care and use of the press. Instructions for handling specific flowers can be found in the "Alphabetic Guide" at the back of the book.

PREPARING THE BORAX MATTRESS

The borax inside the mattress must be loose and free of lumps before the flowers are laid down. Moisture from the air as well as from the flowers previously pressed on the mattress will cause the borax to cake.

With a hammer or block of wood, break up the caked borax. When it has returned to its original granule form, run a ruler across the top of the mattress to redistribute the borax and to smooth the top of the mattress.

DUSTING THE FLOWERS WITH CHALK

The flowers must be dusted with chalk before they enter the press. Mix different chalk pigments to match the natural color of the flowers as closely as possible. To color the flowers, you can

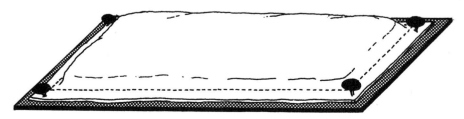

Illus. 4-20. Fix the borax mattress to the Masonite™ by driving a tack into each corner of the bag.

Illus. 4-21. Flowers that are dried in the borax mattress press must first be dusted with chalk.

brush chalk directly onto the petals. You can also drop flowers into a chalk-filled bowl, cover the bowl, and shake it to distribute the chalk on the petals of the flower (Illus. 4–21). Then remove the flowers from the bowl with tweezers and brush away excess chalk. If you don't do this, chalk caught between the petals will cake and harden when the flowers are dried.

Open the press and lay aside the cover, the polyester double-knit fabric, and the 4″ blanket of polyester fibrefill.

Lay the flowers on the borax mattress according to the instructions given for each specific flower. Some flowers are laid on the press right side up, and others upside down.

Cover the flowers with either the polyester double-knit fabric, the 4″ blanket of polyester fibrefill, or both, according to the instructions for each specific flower.

Place the cover on top of the press.

APPLYING HEAT TO DRY THE FLOWERS

Put the press in an oven with just the pilot for heat.

Add weights to the top of the press according to instructions given for each particular flower. In some cases the weight will be a mere five pounds, in others, 30 pounds. If you don't have a pilot light in your oven, preheat the oven to 100° or so, turn off the oven, and put the press in the warm oven. Repeat this process, if necessary, until the flowers are dry. You cannot use high heat on the flowers, because they will scorch. Tack a note on the front of the oven door so that the family does not forget and attempt to preheat the oven for dinner rolls while the press is in the oven.

If humidity in your house is very low and the house is 70° or more both night and day, the flowers will usually dry well without adding heat.

REMOVING THE FLOWERS FROM THE PRESS

Be careful to slide your fingers well under the flower and support the center of the flower while it is being lifted off the pressing surface. Do not pull on the petals of the flower to remove it from the press.

A dry flower will be stiff and crisp throughout—the petals as well as the center of the flower. If the petals appear limp, the flower has probably not dried completely. Flowers that have not completely dried are sometimes cold to the touch. When a flower that is only partly dried is removed from the press, shrinkage and puckering might result.

Illus. 4-22. The phaleonopsis orchids that make up the upper portion of this bouquet could not have been preserved in such near perfect condition without the borax mattress press.

CARE OF THE BORAX MATTRESS

The borax mattress should be stored in a dry area, up off the floor, to prevent moisture from collecting in the borax granules. Vacuum the surface of the mattress and shake the double-knit fabric to remove the excess chalk. From time to time, the double-knit fabric may need to be washed. Any stains of chalk left on the mattress or double-knit fabric will not affect the color of flowers subsequently pressed on the mattress.

CARE OF THE POLYESTER FIBREFILL BLANKET

After the polyester fibrefill blanket has been used several times on the press, it will need to be replaced. The old blanket can be used for mounting pressed-flower pictures and wedding bouquets, as it is the same quality as that used to pad the back of the pictures.

The Microwave Oven

Many times, a microwave oven is used as a time-saving device, quickly drying a flower that would normally spend a week in the basic press. And indeed, the microwave oven is a handy convenience for those times when you might be inspired at the last minute to decorate a gift package with pressed flowers. But in some cases, a microwave oven is more than a convenience. It is essential for successfully pressing certain flowers and leaves, such as mum daisies, cymbidium and dendrobium orchids (Illus. 4–23), stephanotis, algerian ivy, and asparagus fern. (See the "Alphabetic Guide" for other species.)

Described here is only a general outline for microwaving flowers. When pressing a particular flower, always follow the instructions under that entry in the Alphabetic Guide. Do not guess. For perfect results, these flowers must be handled exactly as described in the guide.

Illus. 4-23. Delicate flowers, such as the lovely cymbidium orchids in this display, must be dried in a microwave oven. They would discolor during the several hours that it would normally take for them to dry in a conventional oven.

DUSTING THE FLOWERS WITH CHALK

Before flowers can be pressed in the microwave, they must be dusted with chalk. Chalk accelerates drying and prevents discoloration.

After coating the flower with chalk mixed to match the color of the live flower, brush the excess chalk from the flower and prepare as usual—a plain sheet of chipboard against the face of the flower and padded pressboard against the back of the flower. The sandwich should be sparsely filled.

Press only one sandwich of flowers at a time in a microwave oven. Additional sandwiches will slow down the action of the microwaves.

WEIGHTS FOR PRESSURE

Use only a block of marble or a glass object to weigh down the top of the sandwich of flowers. Brick or pottery objects, which have pockets of air in them, interrupt the flow of the microwaves, preventing them from reaching the flowers. Glass and marble are solid masses, and microwaves pass right through these materials.

It is advisable to have on hand three or four blocks of marble when pressing a long series of sandwiches because a continuously used block of marble will soon become too hot to handle.

TIMING

Follow the instructions given in the Alphabetic Guide.

CORNSTARCH

Do not use cornstarch when pressing flowers in a microwave oven. The cornstarch will cook onto the moist flowers.

Pressing Simple Garden Flowers

Almost any flower can be pressed in a microwave oven. For simple garden flowers, prepare the flower in the usual way. Place the front of the flower against the plain chipboard sheet and cover the back of the flower with the padded pressboard. Place the flowers close together but not touching. Unlike microwave-essential flowers, for which sandwiches should be sparsely filled, sandwiches of simple garden flowers can be generously filled. Results can sometimes be disappointing if such a sandwich is only sparsely filled. Again, press only one sandwich of flowers at a time.

WEIGHTS FOR PRESSURE

As stated previously, use only a block of marble or a heavy glass object.

TIMING FOR STURDY FLOWERS

Hardy flowers, such as pansies, larkspurs, or miniature roses, should be microwaved for two minutes on ¾ power. When they are done, let them stand for 30 minutes.

Check to see if the flowers have dried completely. Then microwave them again for ½ minute on ¾ power. Let them stand for 10 minutes.

Slide a thin knife blade under the flowers to release those that may have stuck to either the plain chipboard sheet or to the padded pressboard. Then reclose the sandwich and reapply the pressure.

Keep the flowers under pressure immediately after they have been removed from the microwave oven. If time allows, finish drying flowers in the basic press with heat for about one hour. If not, microwave again at ½ minute intervals and let stand for 10 minutes.

When drying in the microwave oven, always allow for standing time between shots.

TIMING FOR THIN DELICATE FLOWERS

Some thin, delicate flowers, such as phlox or lobelia, can become permanently fused to the chipboard when dried at ¾ power for two minutes. Timing for these flowers should be adjusted to one minute at ¾ power. Then finish drying them for about one hour in the basic press with heat.

Pressing Leaves and Fern in a Microwave Oven

Leaves and fern dry more quickly in a microwave oven than do flowers. As a result, two or more sandwiches of leaves can be dried in a microwave oven at the same time. Microwave leaves for one minute on ¾ power and leave standing for two minutes. Check them before returning the sandwich to the microwave, because some leaves will dry in only one minute. Leaves are dry when their stems are brittle and snap off with a cracking sound. If they are not yet dry, return the sandwich to the microwave oven for one-minute intervals on ¾ power as required until the leaves are crisp and dry.

Shortcomings of the Microwave Oven

Microwave ovens are indispensable for drying certain flowers and leaves as well as for situations where speed is an advantage, but you should be aware of some of the disadvantages a microwave oven can present.

When using a microwave oven, you cannot control for shrinkage, which can reduce a flower or leaf to ⅞ of its original size. However, shrinkage is not a bad trade-off to pay for increased color retention in those flowers that tolerate no other pressing method. In some cases, shrinkage might even be an advantage. Very large leaves, such as those of the dieffenbachia and the maranta, can be used in a wedding bouquet to a better advantage after a bit of shrinkage has taken place.

Neither leatherleaf fern nor rabbit's-foot fern should be dried in a microwave oven. Shrinkage distorts the fullness of these plants, leaving large spaces between leaflets.

The same holds true for coreopsis flowers. Shrinkage results in large unattractive spaces between the petals of these full-petalled flowers.

Brittleness is also a problem when using a microwave. Some flowers become very brittle after they have been subjected to microwaves, making them difficult to handle. This can be controlled by removing the flower from the microwave oven just before it is totally dried and completing its drying cycle in the basic press.

The many-layered petals of some flowers, such as marigolds, fuse together when dried in a microwave, forming a solid, unattractive blob. It is best not to use a microwave oven for multi-petalled flowers.

Another surprising disadvantage of the microwave oven can be time because you can only press one sandwich at a time. Although each sandwich of flowers requires only two minutes, a series of 20 sandwiches at two minutes each can keep you occupied for 40 minutes.

5

Mounting Flowers on Paper

Flowers and leaves used for this craft should be thin. Because the flowers will be used for only a short time, their durability of color need not be a consideration. Felt-pen ink can be applied when brightly colored flowers are needed. Colorful flowers that are too large for paper goods can be cut into shapes and used to create contrived flowers.

Gluing Flowers

First, slightly dilute some tacky glue to loosen up its gummy quality. Then, brush the glue directly onto the paper. Position a flower on the paper and press down on it with a clean finger in order to firmly seat the flower on the paper. If you have glued a multipetalled flower to the paper, run a dab of glue between the loose petals of the flower. Press down on the petals to firmly glue them together.

Gluing Leaves

Use tacky quickset glue at full strength when gluing leaves to paper. Dip the back of the leaf in a puddle of glue and then drag the leaf across a clean paper surface to remove the excess glue. Position the leaf on the paper and press down on it.

Stationery

Simple, elegant stationery is easy to make using pressed flowers glued directly onto the paper. Correspondence, invitations, thank-you notes, and announcements all take on special meaning when they are decorated with pressed flowers.

Choose a good quality paper with a hard finish in a color that is complementary to the flowers to be used in the design. Soft absorbent paper is too easily stained if glue squeezes out from under the flowers. If the envelope flap is to be decorated with flowers, select stationery that does not have the manufacturer's name embossed on the flap.

Although you can place flowers anywhere you wish, the upper right and lower left hand corners are probably the most practical because these areas will not interfere with the salutation or the signature. Measure and lightly mark fold lines on the stationery before planning a design to avoid applying flowers in that area.

A few decorative lines (Illus. 5–1) will enhance an otherwise simple arrangement of flowers. For accuracy in lining up the graphics with the flowers, draw lines on the stationery after the flowers have been glued onto the paper. Learn to use a draftsman's triangle so that you can draw lines that are parallel to the edge of the paper. French-curve templates should be used for accuracy when adding curved lines.

Illus. 5-1. Decorating stationery with dried, pressed flowers is quick and easy—a perfect project for a beginner.

Gift Wrap and Gift Tags

Paper for gift wrap should be of fairly heavy weight to ensure that the glue does not bleed through the paper and stick to the box below. Papers with a slick finish afford a better surface for removing excess glue from around the flowers. When selecting paper and ribbon to match or complement the flowers and leaves used on the package, carry with you samples of the pressed materials. Avoid brightly colored paper and ribbon, which might clash with the more delicate, muted shades of the plant materials.

GLUE

For this craft, use rubber cement. Apply glue first to the back of the flower, and then apply the flower to the paper. After the glue has dried, any small amount of rubber cement that might show around the edges of the flowers and leaves can be removed by gently rubbing it with either your finger or with a rubber cement eraser until the glue rolls up into a nice neat little ball. Although tacky white glue can be substituted for rubber cement, cleanup around the edges of the vegetation is not possible.

CHOOSING FLOWERS FOR GIFT WRAP

Flowers and leaves that are sturdy, large, and readily available are the best choice. They should be sturdy so that they hold up well during the gluing process, large for high visibility, and readily available because the time invested in growing the flowers should be commensurate with their short-term use.

Smaller versions of stationery or greeting cards can be made for use as gift tags by matching the flowers on the tag with those used on the gift wrap.

Place Cards

Place cards decorated with pressed flowers can enhance any table setting on special occasions. Choose a paper or card stock that is heavy enough to stand when folded in half and is of a color that complements the flowers and china. The card should be of a quality that does not allow ink to bleed when graphics are drawn.

Lightly mark a fold line with a pencil so that you can keep the design on the front of the card. With colored pens, you can draw a border all around the card before the flowers are glued to it. Decorative lines that tie in close to the flowers

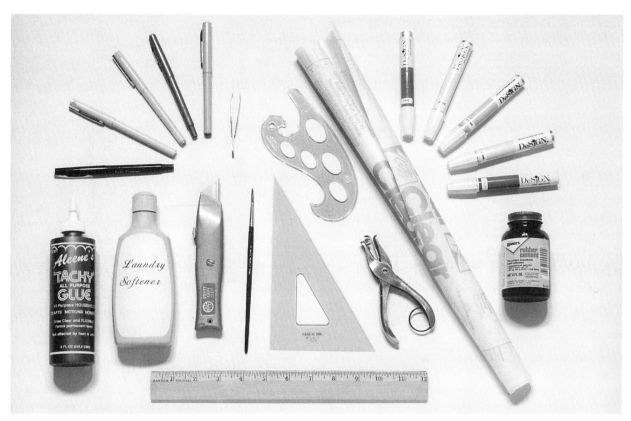

SUPPLIES FOR PAPER GOODS
Illus. 5–2. From top left, clockwise: colored ballpoint pens, French curve template, and felt pens are used to draw graphics on stationery. Rubber cement is used to glue flowers to gift wrap. Flowers can be affixed to greeting cards and bookmarks with plastic laminating film. A hole punch is useful when making holes for ribbon ties on bookmarks. A draftsman's triangle and ruler are helpful when drawing straight lines. A brush is needed to apply glue, and a utility knife can be used to trim edges of the paper. Laundry softener, when applied to plastic film, will counteract static electricity, which often causes flowers to jump out of place as the plastic approaches them. Tacky glue is used to attach flowers directly to paper.

must be drawn after the flowers are glued in place. Use a draftsman's triangle for accuracy when drawing straight lines. If your handwriting is not of the best, use gold or black stick-on letters that are available at stationery stores.

Photo Mounts

Photo mounts can be attractively decorated with a pressed-flower design by gluing the flowers directly onto the heavy paper mat. If the picture is to be mounted in a frame equipped with narrow metal or wood channels along either side, center

the photo in the opening and tape it to the back of the decorated mat. Cover the decorated mat with the glass and slide the three pieces, with glass over the flowers, into the frame. This will keep the flowers from being damaged.

Albums and Scrapbooks

Pressed flowers, glued directly onto the paper pages of an album, can be used to decorate a baby's record book, a guest register, or a bride's memory book. Flowers inside a closed book hold their color much longer than flowers constantly exposed to light. The more perishable colors of pansies could be used successfully in this application. Where facing pages are decorated with flowers, insert a sheet of tissue between the pages.

Keepsakes

Wedding invitations, baby announcements, or mementos of other sorts can be encircled with an arrangement of pressed flowers and framed (Illus. 5–3) as a treasured keepsake of an important occasion.

Lightly glue the invitation to the background fabric with a very small amount of glue. Arrange flowers around the invitation, allowing the flowers to hug the edges of the invitation, spill over on top of the invitation, or peek out from behind. Mount the completed memento as you would a pressed-flower picture.

Illus. 5-3. A wedding invitation can be turned into a treasured keepsake with the addition of a photo mat, some pressed flowers, and a decorative frame.

6
Mounting Flowers with Plastic Laminating Film

Pressed flowers can be sealed onto greeting cards, bookmarks, or the covers of books with plastic laminating film. For this craft, flowers can be a little thicker than those simply glued on paper. In some styles of greeting cards, the flowers are framed in an oval die-cut opening. In others, the embossed margin of an announcement folder gives the completed design a framed effect.

Sheets of heavyweight, glossy-finished laminating film are available in most stationery stores. Lightweight rolls of laminating film are available in houseware departments where shelf paper is sold. The lightweight type of film has a dull finish. Either film is suitable for greeting cards. However, only the more pliable lightweight plastic film can be used to cover books.

Both types of film have a protective backing that must be removed before the film is applied to the flowers. In areas where humidity is low, friction will cause static electricity to gather on the film as the backing is removed. This in turn will cause the flowers to jump out of place as the film approaches them. Rub a small amount of antistatic laundry softener onto the plastic surface of the film before the backing is removed to deactivate the static electricity.

Greeting Cards with Oval Die-Cut Opening

This type of card normally has three panels. The middle panel has an oval window opening, one of the sides panels holds the pressed flowers, and the other side panel serves as the back cover of the card (Illus. 6–1). Before starting to create a design for these cards, be sure you are using the correct panel for the flowers so that the completed card will open in the proper direction.

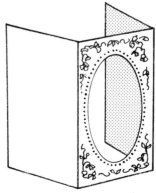

Illus. 6-1. Die-cut greeting cards are perfect venues for pressed-flower arrangements.

51

The size of the design must be kept within the area of the oval window of the card. Do not use glue. When the design has been completed to your satisfaction, cut a piece of the plastic laminating film that is a little larger than the window in the card. Rub fabric softener on the plastic film to deactivate the static electricity.

Remove the protective paper backing from the film and lay it on top of the flowers. Press down on the film to seal the flowers in place.

Fold the window down over the flower arrangement and glue it in place with tacky glue.

Cut a piece of folded writing paper to fit inside the card and fix the paper to the inside with a dab of glue along the spine of the card.

Announcement Folder Greeting Cards

With the card folded, arrange the flowers on the front cover. The flowers need not be glued in place.

Cut a piece of laminating film about 1″ larger than the overall size of the folder. Rub fabric softener on the plastic surface of the film to prevent the flowers from jumping out of place as the plastic approaches them.

Remove the paper backing from the plastic film and bring the film down on the flowers. Press down on the film to seal the flowers in place. At this point, the film will cover the surface of the card unevenly, so simply trim away the excess on all four sides of the card.

Bookmarks

Instructions are given here for two styles of bookmarks: a medallion style, which dangles outside a book and a panel style, which lies inside a book.

MEDALLION

For the medallion, gather a series of bottle or jar lids of three sizes, to serve as templates (Illus.

6–2). The largest circle, which should measure approximately 2″ in diameter, will serve as the cutting guide. The next two sizes, one ⅛″ smaller and one ¼″ smaller, are to be used as guides to draw a border around the flower design. For a beginner, a simple design consisting of a single flower surrounded by leaves is appropriate. A more difficult design, one using tiny flowers and leaves, would be appropriate for a more experienced artisan.

Illus. 6-2. Using different-sized jar tops for templates, cut out three cardboard circles as pictured above. These will serve as patterns for your medallion bookmark design.

Flowers used in a medallion bookmark should be thin. Thick flowers, leaves, or stems in an area as small as this would prevent the plastic film from bonding well along the edge of the paper.

On heavyweight paper, about 3″ square and of a suitable color, trace in pencil an outline of the largest lid. Draw a "U"-shaped tab on top of the circle that is large enough for a hole to be punched into it. This will be used as an anchor on which to tie a narrow ribbon. Erase the pencil mark at the base of the tab.

Center the next smaller lid in the circle that has been drawn on the paper. Trace the outer border around the lid with a pen of a suitable color.

Center the smallest lid in the circle and trace around the lid with a pen of either the same color as the outer border or of a complementary color.

Arrange the flowers inside the smallest circle.

Cut two pieces of laminating film, each about 3″ square, and rub a bit of laundry softener on them. Remove the backing from one piece and cover flowers with it. Press down on the film to seal the flowers in place.

Remove the backing from the second piece of laminating film and apply it to the back of the medallion.

Cut out the medallion along the pencilled guide. Punch a hole in the center of the tab and draw a ribbon through the hole. Even up the ends of the ribbon and tie them in a knot around the tab.

Illus. 6-3. Plastic laminating film can be used to apply pressed-flower designs to many things, including address books and medallion and panel bookmarks (at right).

PANEL BOOKMARK

First choose a sheet of paper in a color to complement the flowers that will be used in the design. Then draw a very lightly pencilled outline of the bookmark—2½″ × 7¾″. With a colored ballpoint pen, draw vertical and horizontal lines parallel to the edges of the bookmark. The longest vertical line should be 4½″ long and each succeeding line ⅜″ shorter. The longest horizontal line should be 1¾″ long. Learn to use a draftsman's triangle to draw straight lines that are parallel with the paper's edge. You may draw small curved lines to connect the ends of each straight line.

Arrange a design of flowers, leaves, and vine tendrils down the length of the panel. Avoid using thick flowers, leaves, or stems, which could prevent the plastic film from bonding well along the edge of the paper. Because panel bookmarks will be enclosed in a book most of the time, the flowers will not fade as quickly as flowers that are always exposed to light. Flowers with less durable color are appropriate here.

Cut a piece of plastic film about 1″ larger than the bookmark. Rub a dab of laundry softener on the plastic film, remove its protective backing, and lay it over the flowers.

Cut out the bookmark along the pencilled guidelines. Then glue the panel to a second piece of heavy paper, in a contrasting or complementary color, that is approximately ³⁄₁₆″ larger than the panel holding the flowers.

Covered Book

Address and appointment books, a local telephone directory, or any book can be decorated with pressed flowers, provided the binding is paper and not plastic. In this craft, the entire book is covered with plastic laminating film, sealing both flowers and book in plastic.

First of all, paper of a suitable color must be glued over the book's original cover. The new cover must be cut to fit across the front, over the spine, and across the back cover. If a border is planned, this should be drawn, using a draftsman's triangle for a guide, before the paper is glued to the book.

Working with the book closed, spread slightly diluted tacky glue evenly over the front cover of the book. Lay one end of the paper over the front cover, making sure that all edges of the new cover and the old cover are even.

Next, spread tacky glue evenly over the spine of the book. Turn the book upside down and

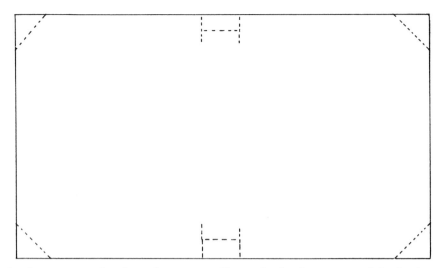

Illus. 6-4. For a book cover, cut the plastic laminating film to fit the dimensions of the book, according to the diagram above.

gently pull the paper over the spine, creasing the paper along its sharp edges. Finally, spread glue on the back cover and glue the new back cover in place.

After the glue has dried, the flowers can be arranged on the front cover. All the pressed material must be firmly glued in place so that plastic film can be applied. During this process, the book will be turned over on its side, flowers and all, so the vegetation must be firmly anchored to the book cover.

To cover the book with plastic laminating film, cut a piece of film an inch or two larger (depending upon the size of the book) than the overall measurement of the book. Lay the film over the book and cut two slits in it at the spine of the book. Clip away enough film at the four corners to make neat, fitted corners (Illus. 6–4). To counteract static electricity, rub laundry softener on the plastic before removing the paper backing. As an extra precaution, I also rub the softener on my hands and on the workbench.

Remove the backing from the plastic laminating film, and lay the film, sticky side up, on the workbench. After cutting away the excess film, fold the flaps to form a finished edge where the channels were cut for the spine. Lay the front of the book face down on top of the sticky film, lining up the spine with the channels.

To overlap the film to the inside of the cover, keep the front cover down on the table, open up all the other pages, and rub the film down against the inside surface of the front cover. Be sure to line up the fitted corners.

Roll the book over so that the back of the book is against the sticky film, turn, and rub the film down against the inside surface of the back cover.

Cloth-Covered Book

You can also create a cloth-covered book with a framed display of pressed flowers sealed under plastic laminating film. I have included instructions for a cloth-covered photograph album.

THE FLOWER ARRANGEMENT

For this, you must first purchase a 5″ × 7″ heavyweight oval picture mat. These are available where frames or art supplies are sold.

Next, cut a piece of background fabric, in the color of your choice, about one inch larger than the oval opening in the mat.

Lay the oval mat over the fabric, and then arrange the flowers on the cloth within the area of the opening. Allow a good margin of space between the flower arrangement and the edge of the oval.

To seal the flower arrangement in plastic, re-move the mat and cut a piece of laminating film the same size as the cloth. Rub a dab of laundry softener on the plastic film, remove the backing, and cover the flowers with the laminating film.

Set the arrangement aside.

THE 5″ × 7″ PICTURE MAT

Using the oval picture mat for a pattern, cut polyester fibrefill padding the same size as the mat (Illus. 6–5). Glue the padding to the mat.

Lay a piece of fabric over the padded mat. Draw the fabric around to the back of the mat and cut the fabric 2″ larger than the size of the mat. Then glue the edges of the fabric to the back of the mat, cutting away excess fabric as neces-sary to make neatly fitted corners.

Starting with two small crisscross slits in the center of the fabric, cut a hole where the center of the oval opening is located. Extend the slits to within ½″ of the edge of the mat opening.

Pull the slitted fabric edges down through the mat opening and glue them to the back of the picture mat (Illus. 6–6), cutting the slits deeper or removing excess fabric as necessary.

Glue lace trim and/or pearls around the oval opening.

Set the covered picture mat aside.

COVERING THE BOOK

With the book closed, wrap fabric completely around it. Cut the fabric 1″ larger than the over-all measurement of the book when it is closed.

Using tacky glue, turn in the overlapping 1″ of fabric and glue it inside the covers of the book (Illus. 6–7), cutting away excess material at the spine and the corners as necessary to make neat corners.

Cut two equal lengths of ribbon and glue them to the book—one to the front cover, and another to the back cover.

Set the book aside.

INSIDE COVER OF THE BOOK

From a piece of lightweight poster board, cut two rectangles ¼″ smaller than the inside covers of the book.

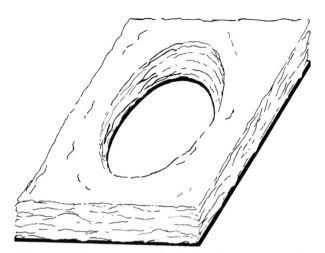

Illus. 6-5. To create a quilted effect for the cover of the cloth-covered book, cut a polyester pad the same size and shape as the picture mat.

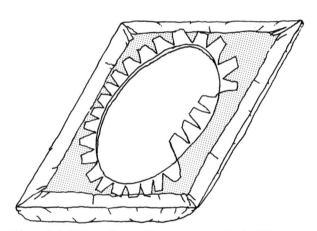

Illus. 6-6. Wrap the padding and mat with fabric, glue the cloth down, and cut out the opening for the flower arrangement. Then pull the fabric through the opening and glue it down.

Cut the fabric ½″ larger than the rectangles of poster board. Cover the rectangles with fabric, gluing the extra ½″ of fabric to their undersides, making sure that the corners are neatly fitted.

Set inside covers aside.

ASSEMBLING THE BOOK

Center the sealed flower arrangement on the front of the photograph album and glue it in place by dabbing spots of glue around the outer edges of the cloth.

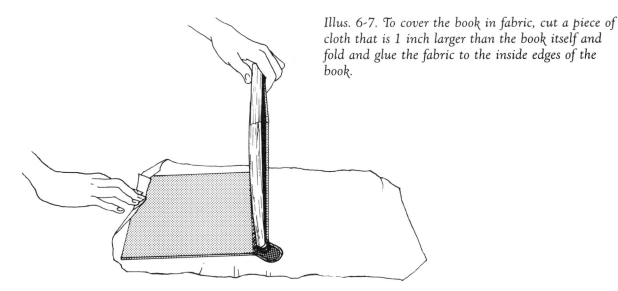

Illus. 6-7. To cover the book in fabric, cut a piece of cloth that is 1 inch larger than the book itself and fold and glue the fabric to the inside edges of the book.

Center the upholstered picture mat over the flower arrangement and glue it to the front cover of the book.

Open the book and glue lace trim along the inside edge of the cover, allowing it to protrude beyond the edge of the book.

Glue the two covered rectangles of poster board to the inside covers of the book, covering up the raw edges of lace along the inside edge of the book.

Specialties Manufactured for Pressed-Flower Designs

Some manufacturers have equipped several useful and interesting objects with fittings for displaying pressed-flower designs (Illus. 6–8). Included here are instructions for a box, a tray, a pendant, and a dressing table set.

BOX

Dismantle the box. Cut a piece of background fabric that is the same size as the sponge supplied by the manufacturer. Lay the background fabric over the sponge and arrange the flowers on it, gluing them to the fabric with the tiniest spots of glue.

Apply antistatic laundry softener to the plastic cover and reassemble the box according to the manufacturer's instructions.

PENDANT

Dismantle the pendant. Cut a piece of background fabric the same size as the oval insert supplied by the manufacturer. Arrange and glue the flowers on the fabric with glue. Apply antistatic laundry softener to the plastic window of the pendant and reassemble according to the manufacturer's instructions.

DRESSING TABLE SET

Mirror: Dismantle the mirror. Cut a piece of background fabric 1″ larger than the paddle, using as a pattern the cardboard filler supplied by the manufacturer. For padding, cut one or two pieces of cotton flannel slightly smaller than the cardboard filler.

Glue the flannel pieces to the metal paddle. Wrap the background fabric over the flannel and tape it to the back of the paddle. Arrange the flowers and leaves on the background fabric, gluing each in place with a tiny spot of glue.

Apply antistatic laundry softener to the plastic cover and reassemble the mirror as directed by

Illus. 6-8. Several manufacturers have created household objects equipped with display areas for pressed-flower arrangements. Pictured here is a vanity table set.

the manufacturer, removing the cardboard fillers as necessary.

Brush: Dismantle the brush. Cut a piece of background fabric and two pieces of flannel for padding, all the same size as the top of the brush. Arrange and glue the flowers on the background fabric. Apply antistatic laundry softener to the plastic cover and reassemble the brush as directed by the manufacturer.

Tray: Dismantle the tray. Cut a piece of background fabric and a piece of flannel padding the same size as the insert supplied with the tray. Arrange the flowers on the background. Glue will not be necessary. Cover the arrangement with the glass that is permanently affixed to the frame of the tray. Turn the tray upside down and glue the cover to the back of the tray.

7

Mounting Flowers on Wooden Objects

Any wooden object can be decorated with pressed flowers. By trimming, altering, and manipulating the flowers, you can create any style you might want for the decor of a particular room.

Repetition is a particularly effective technique for this type of decorating. You can arrange petals so that they march around the lid of the box or along the top of a piece of furniture. A border of flowers, leaves, or petals might frame a spray of flowers arranged at the middle of a drawer front.

Flowers for this craft should be thin and have good color retention or have color added with felt-pen ink.

The objects used in this craft should be of new wood. An unblemished surface will afford you an opportunity to apply the paint or stain of your choice, so that the finish will make a positive impact on the design. There are paints, stains, and finishes of every imaginable color. Experiment with some of the available colors in combination with the flowers to be used in the design and choose one that provides the best setting.

Preparing the Surface

Sand all the surfaces with fine sandpaper and apply paint or stain in the desired color according to the manufacturer's instructions. For a clear finish, leave the wood unfinished until the flowers are ready to arrange on the surface. For a stained finish, apply one coat of clear finish to the stain before applying the flowers. Do not arrange flowers close to the edges. A protective margin of wood must be allowed in order to prevent chipping.

Applying Flowers

Brush clear finish only on the area to be decorated with flowers. Apply the flowers and leaves while the surface is wet, so that their positions can be manipulated for a short time. The plant materials will slide easily on the freshly varnished surface, but use caution to avoid tearing the petals from the smaller, more delicate blossoms. Gently press down on the vegetation with a blunt wooden object or with the eraser end of a pencil to firmly seat the pieces in place. If the flowers used in the design are multipetalled, run a little of the clear finish under the petals where they overlap. There should be no pockets of air under the flowers or leaves.

Allow the finish to dry thoroughly.

If you are decorating more than one surface of the object with flowers, complete one surface and allow the flowers to dry thoroughly before moving on to the next surface.

Sealing the Flowers

When all the surfaces have been decorated, spray or brush several coats of clear finish over the entire object to seal in the flowers. Allow each coat to dry thoroughly and sand it lightly with very fine sandpaper before applying successive coats. Use caution when sanding where flowers are mounted.

When the work is completed, the flowers should be completely embedded in the clear finish. Any flowers or leaves with rough, uncovered, or thinly covered edges will in time chip away as the object is handled.

Illus. 7-1. Wooden objects, such as this box, provide ideal surfaces for pressed-flower arrangements. All you need are some flowers, sandpaper, and clear varnish.

8

Mounting and Framing Pressed-Flower Pictures

A pressed-flower picture consists of seven parts (Illus. 8–1): frame, glass, flowers, background fabric, polyester fibrefill padding, rigid backboard, and back cover.

The Frame

Some frames are suitable for pressed-flower pictures, but others are not. One feature that must be considered when choosing a frame is whether or not a staple can be driven through the back of the frame to firmly fasten the picture.

WOOD FRAMES

A common paper stapler can be used to attach the back cover to most wood frames. One exception is very hard oak. Some oak frames are so hard that holes must be drilled into the back of the frame for screws.

COMPOSITION FRAMES

These frames are made from a hard, rubber-like material. Most are molded into oval shapes and can be found at reasonable prices. Only staples with legs ⅛″ apart and ³⁄₁₆″ long will hold securely in this material.

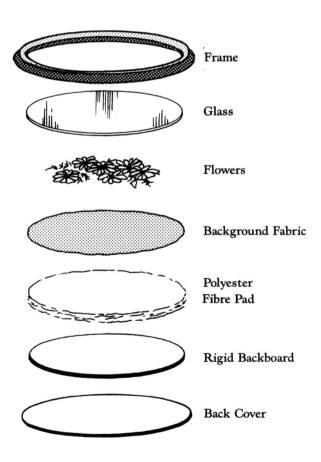

Frame

Glass

Flowers

Background Fabric

Polyester Fibre Pad

Rigid Backboard

Back Cover

Illus. 8-1. The seven parts that make up a pressed-flower picture.

METAL AND PLASTIC FRAMES

Metal and plastic frames can sometimes be found equipped with a backing secured with clamps so the back of the frame can be opened and closed. These are very convenient for pressed-flower pictures. Each is already equipped with a rigid backboard firmly clamped to the back of the frame. Metal and plastic frames not equipped in this way cannot be used because there is no way to fasten the picture into the frame.

PHOTOGRAPH FRAMES

Frames that have channels on either side into which photographs must be slid are unsuitable because the flowers are disturbed as the arrangement slides into the frame.

Other features to keep in mind when choosing a frame are its dimensions (Illus. 8–2). There are three dimensions that are most important to consider. The first is the size of the lip where the glass will rest. When the lip of a frame is a scant ¼″ wide (some are even less), it is difficult to keep the edges of the background fabric from showing. Also, there is no allowance for movement of the fabric during framing. A lip of at least ⅜″ is advisable.

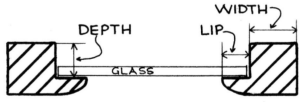

Illus. 8-2. When choosing a frame for a pressed-flower picture, you must make sure that the dimensions are suitable, particularly the depth of the picture opening.

The second dimension to bear in mind is the width of the moulding.

This measurement should be around ¾″. Half an inch is not really very useful. Moulding that is less than ¾″ wide is acceptable, but requires more precision in cutting and fitting the cover across the back of the frame.

The third and last dimension to consider is the depth of the picture opening. This should be around ⅜″—deep enough to hold the ⅛″-thick

glass, the ⅛″-thick backboard, and the thick pad of polyester fibrefill. Although it is possible to use frames with less depth, a bulge in the back of the picture will be evident when padding has been forced into a tight enclosure.

Glass

Ordinary window glass, cut to fit inside the frame, can be used for pressed-flower pictures. Non-glare glass, which may appeal to some, tends to alter the appearance of the fabrics, making all types take on the dull appearance of felt.

Background Fabric

Flowers must be mounted against a piece of soft, pliable fabric. Stiff fabrics will wrinkle, and puckers will appear where thick parts of the flowers are pressed against the fabric.

The fabric should be cut exactly the same size as the glass. If the fabric is larger than the piece of glass, the extra margin of fabric, pushing against the edge of the frame, can cause the flat part of the fabric to pucker.

POLYESTER DRESS FABRICS

Soft, pliable polyester dress materials that have a reasonable amount of body will accommodate flowers very well and are available in many colors. Thin fabrics that drape well are generally more difficult to work. Polyester double knits are too coarse, and fabrics with embossed woven patterns will, over time, transfer onto the petals of the flowers.

VELVET

Panne velvet is a soft fabric that drapes well and has a nap that runs in one direction. It is an excellent fabric for pressed-flower pictures. The flowers sink into the velvet nap, giving them added support. Though velveteen also has a nap running in one direction, its backing is very stiff and thick, almost like canvas, and therefore unsuitable for backgrounds.

Conventional velvet is also unsuitable for pressed-flower pictures because the nap on this fabric stands on end. When the glass is pressed against it, the nap is crushed, causing color changes where pressure from the glass is heaviest.

SATIN, TAFFETA, AND BROADCLOTH

None of these fabrics work well in pressed-flower pictures. Satin is not a fabric for beginners. Though very attractive, it is difficult to work with because the flowers slide out of place too easily. Taffeta and broadcloth are stiff unyielding fabrics, not pliable enough for pressed-flower pictures.

Polyester Fibrefill

A backing pad of polyester fibrefill must be cut to the same size as the glass in the frame and it should be of a generous thickness and of absolutely no sizing.

Backboard

A rigid backboard must be cut the same size as the glass to fit inside the frame behind the polyester pad. Thin poster board or corrugated cardboard is not sufficiently rigid to serve as a backboard. Canvas boards sold for oil painting are excellent rigid materials for making backboards. They are sold in all standard rectangular frame sizes and can be cut to fit oval frames with the sharp blade of a utility knife or a jigsaw.

Back Cover

This cover, which will fit across the back of the frame, must be cut out of a stiff piece of poster board. It should be cut slightly smaller than the overall size of the frame so that it will not show along the edges when the picture is hung on the wall.

Arranging and Mounting Flowers

Place the fabric right side up directly on top of the glass. Arrange the flowers on the fabric using a tweezer (Illus. 8–3). See the section on design for suggested placement of the flowers.

Illus. 8-3. Arrange flowers on the fabric background with tweezers. Always keep the glass underneath the fabric while arranging.

When all the flowers are in place, center the polyester pad on the rigid backboard (Illus. 8–4). Then, gently pick up the glass with the flower arrangement and background fabric and hold the glass over the polyester pad. Slide the glass out from under the fabric, transferring the fabric and the arrangement of flowers completely intact onto the polyester pad (Illus. 8–5). (When making a large piece, the weight of the fabric should be taken into account. Thin fabrics with very little body tend to be more difficult to transfer to the polyester pad.)

Next, wash and dry the glass and place it over the flowers (Illus. 8–6).

Then, fit the frame over the glass (Illus. 8–7).

Slide the picture to the edge of the table and grasp the picture in both hands. Press down with your thumbs on the top edge of the frame, and reach underneath with your fingers to press up firmly against the backboard (Illus. 8–8).

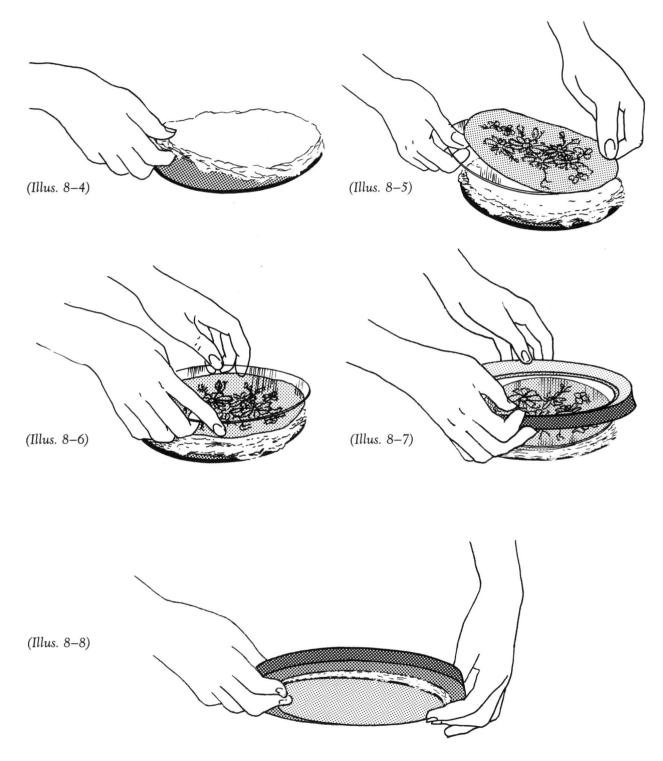

(Illus. 8–4)

(Illus. 8–5)

(Illus. 8–6)

(Illus. 8–7)

(Illus. 8–8)

Illus. 8-4 through 8-8. Follow these steps to frame your arrangement: Place the polyester pad on the backboard, hold the glass and arrangement over the pad and slide the glass out from under the fabric. Then cover the arrangement with the glass, cover the glass with the frame, and push the backboard into the frame.

Carefully turn the picture upside down onto a padded surface to protect the finish on the frame.

Apply tacky white glue around the back of the frame (Illus. 8–9).

Fit the back cover onto the back of the frame and staple it to the frame (Illus. 8–10). Make certain that the rigid backboard is fitted down inside the opening of the frame, pressing down on the pad of polyester fibrefill.

ter the picture has been completed and framed.

To start, turn the picture upside down on a padded surface and remove the back cover and rigid backboard. Very carefully lift the polyester fibrefill padding off the back of the fabric. Do not remove the frame.

Starting at one end of the picture, slowly peel back the fabric, all the while watching for vegetation that might stick to the fabric. Gently coax

Illus. 8-9 and 8-10. Apply glue to the back moulding of the frame, glue the back cover on, and staple it in place.

If you plan to bring a picture to a frame shop to select an appropriate setting there, you should secure the arrangement with very large clamps to ensure its safety while enroute.

Complete the mounting process as described, up to the placement of the glass. Use clamps large enough to allow one flange to grip the glass and the other to reach under the arrangement to grip the heavy backboard.

Changing Background Fabric

Though not easy and requiring a steady hand (and nerves of steel), it is possible to change the fabric background in a pressed-flower picture af-

the vegetation off the fabric so that it falls back onto the glass before proceeding. You will be able to see the back of the flowers lying upside down against the clear glass.

After lifting half of the fabric background off the flowers, carefully lower that piece of fabric down on top of the remaining half of the fabric. The background fabric will now be folded in half and cover only one half of the flower arrangement.

Roll the folded end back, uncovering more of the back of the arrangement. Be careful not to allow the fabric to slide, because the vegetation will be pushed out of position. Continue rolling the fabric up until it can be picked up off the last part of the arrangement.

Then cut a new piece of fabric and fold it in half, right side out. Carefully lay the folded piece of fabric over one half of the arrangement. Turn

A memento book with flowers glued directly onto the paper and a cloth-covered photo album with a mounted pressed-flower arrangement (top). The pink cattleya orchid, red roses, and pansies in these designs (left) were all colored with either chalk or felt-pen ink.

A

A crescent design of pansies, heather, and fern. This type of arrangement can be embellished as lavishly as you like, so long as the basic lines of the crescent are still visible.

A circle of flowers that includes Johnny-jump-ups, multicaule mums, lobelias, larkspurs, forget-me-nots, Queen Anne's lace, spirea, candytuft, and rose leaves.

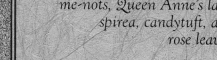

A cascade-style bouquet for which both the carnations and the roses have been pressed in full-face and in profile views to recreate the original shape of the live piece.

A nosegay wedding bouquet of delicate pink roses, baby's breath, and fern that was pressed and arranged on top of the couple's wedding invitation.

A presentation-style wedding bouquet consisting of phaleonopsis and dendrobium orchids, carnations, roses, baby's breath, and maidenhair fern. The groom's boutonniere was also included on the lower right.

A simple nosegay bouquet made with pressed marguerite daisies, heather, Queen Anne's lace, and rabbit's-foot fern. Long pieces of grass hang from the base, giving the illusion of stems.

D

A wedding bouquet that was arranged on top of a simulated prayer book made from index cards and gold ribbon. The stephanotis were pressed in various positions to give the arrangement perspective.

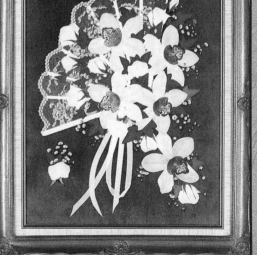

A bouquet that includes cymbidium orchids, white roses, and baby's breath and was arranged on a recreated fan.

E

Flowers and leaves that are sturdy and large are the best choice for decorating gift wrap and greeting cards.

F

Fern that imitates the shape of pine trees was used to give this gift wrap a Christmas-like appearance (top). Left, place cards that have been decorated with pressed flowers can enhance a table for any special occasion.

G

A shoji screen that has flower arrangements pressed between the rice paper sheets in each of its panels.

back a small edge of fabric and lay a weight, such as scissors or a bottle of glue, on the part of the fabric that is against the glass. This will prevent the fabric from moving about as you work. Unfold the fabric, and, by degrees, let it gently fall onto the back of the arrangement until the entire background is in place.

Remove the weight and reposition the polyester fibrefill pad behind the new background fabric. Cover the pad with the rigid backboard. Turn the picture right side up on the workbench and check to see that everything is in place. If anything has slipped, remove the frame and simply slide under the glass a long, flat tool, such as a blunt knife blade or a long, thin screwdriver, and nudge any stray vegetation back into place.

Replace the frame, turn the picture upside down on a padded surface, and proceed as usual, fastening a new cover to the back of the frame.

Mounting Flowers with Glue

Although I usually frown on the practice of gluing flowers onto a background of paper, I must admit to one circumstance where I cast aside my aversion—when it's for money! For craft fairs, I make many simple arrangements using all kinds of flowers, whether durable or not, glue the flowers in place on paper backgrounds, and frame them with just a mat. (Photo mounts are available from photographic supply houses and can be acquired cheaply when purchased in lots of 100.)

Once at the fair, I simply hung out a sign reading "U Frame It" and was rewarded with brisk sales because of the very low price. For speed in production, I repeated several simple designs, using common, abundantly available flowers.

Illus. 8–11. Top left, clockwise: a staple gun with narrow bridge staples is used when closing the back of composition frames, and a stapler with wide bridge staples is used on the back of wood frames. A hammer will be necessary to mount hangers to the back of pictures. You will also need tacky glue to seal the back cover to the frame and a utility knife or scissors to cut the backboard and back cover for the frame. A special paint-like ink will allow you to stamp your signature on the inside surface of the glass.

9

Designing Pressed-Flower Pictures

Before you begin your own pressed-flower pictures, you should consider some of the effects and principles of design and organization that appear in the work of others. The first element to consider is the condition of the flowers themselves. Are they pressed with clean, clear, durable color? Are they free from discoloration, scars, or disfigurements? Is there any trace of shriveling? The petals, even in critical areas at their bases, should not be puckered, distorted, or misshapen.

It is also important to consider the setting or frame surrounding the design. Is a heavy, ornate frame overpowering the subject? The color and style of the frame should be in keeping with the color and style of the design. Is the frame too small, cramping the design? Are plant materials so crowded into their allotted space that they are arranged right up to or caught under the frame? Is the frame too large, causing a tiny design to become lost in a sea of empty space?

A third and equally important element is cohesion. Do the combined elements of form, line, motion, and color hold the design together? Does the arrangement, where appropriate, exhibit a strong center of gravity? Flowers and leaves should not be floating around lost in space, nor should isolated flowers be used simply to fill empty corners of the frame, leaving them with no connection or relationship to the rest of the design.

A design should also be evaluated for its truth to nature. Flowers should not appear to be growing out of a leaf or out of the head of another flower. Tiny embellishments of vine tendrils or buds should emulate believable natural growth habits. There should be no careless additions that have little natural relationship to the adjacent vegetation.

Movement and strong lines are other elements to consider. They can be created by the placement of a succession of flowers, leaves, stems, sprays, or color, which draws the eye through the design. An element of movement gives life and vitality to an arrangement. These qualities can also be achieved by manipulating the blossoms to show depth and perspective. Some of the flowers should appear to be in back of others, others to nod or turn away, and still others to stand straight and tall. The unrelieved monotony of all the flowers displayed full face is reminiscent of little children staring into a candy store window, with their noses pressed flat against the window.

The colors in a pressed-flower design should be judged for their total effect. This should include the impact that the background color makes on a design. It is as much a part of the color scheme as the flowers themselves and should be in balanced harmony with the arrangement, neither overpowering nor upstaging the design. The colors of both the flowers and the background should support the style, line, and motion of a design. Strong color harmony best supports strong bold lines and softer colors produce a gentler effect.

A competent artisan who has taken the time to test color durability of the flowers can visualize changes that will occur as the flowers age. In the choice of flowers used, his or her expertise will be evident after the picture has aged. Indeed, aging can add a dimension that might be an asset to a design. In some flowers, the veins discolor at a more advanced rate than the rest of the petal, revealing a network of intricate and beautiful patterns weaving their way through the petals. This quality will not be apparent in a freshly dried flower.

Pressed-flower pictures have long been known as a Victorian art—an expression of the Victorian age. Seldom do we see a picture that transcends the traditional use of the Victorian theme. A nosegay, crescent, triangle, massed arrangement, or "S" curve are all traditional Victorian designs that use the flowers in the most obvious

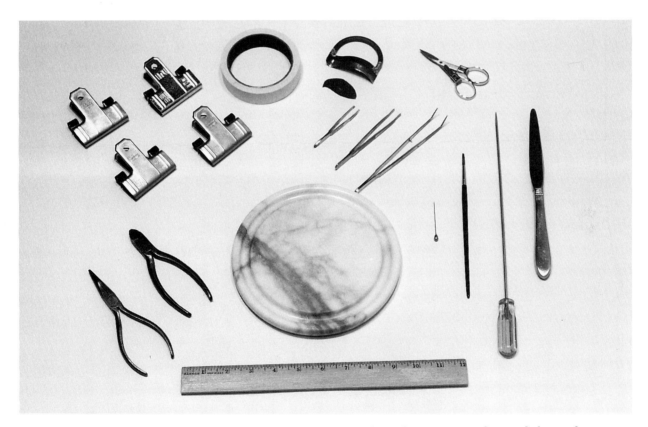

Illus. 9–1. Top left, clockwise: large clamps are used to hold unframed pictures together, and the masking tape is used when reassembling the flowers. A curved cutting tool is useful for cutting curved shapes into petals and leaves, and scissors are needed to trim the flowers. A thin knife blade is handy for coaxing thin delicate flowers off the pressboards. A long-bladed screwdriver can be used to nudge stray flowers into position after the glass has been placed over the arrangement. A brush is used for removing lint and debris from the picture before it is framed, and the tweezers or pin can be used to handle the flowers. The slab of marble is used as a weight when drying flowers in the microwave oven. A ruler should be available to measure bouquets, and wire cutters and long-nosed pliers are needed to cut and remove wires from flowers in wedding bouquets.

way. Though these designs are all legitimate and often very lovely, they are old standards that have been repeated over and over again.

Designs of any kind are possible (Illus. 9–2), and the potential for pressed-flower pictures is limited only by the imagination. However, very little experimentation or adventurous spirit has been shown in the craft. By comparison, its sister art of flower arranging has flourished worldwide, resulting in experimentation, dramatic changes, growth, and maturity. Flower arranging has followed the trends of other mediums of artistic expression—some good, some bad, but never static.

Surrealism, art deco, landscaping, or any other design style born of a vivid imagination is possible in pressed-flower pictures. By using pressed plant materials in unusual ways, petals of flowers can be rearranged to form imaginative baroque or geometric designs, or perhaps we might create an imaginary floral scene of the prehistoric world. One adventurous soul has even succeeded in portraiture by using the delicate shadings and colors of pressed plant materials as his medium. All the features and shadows of the subject's face were visible and recognizable, although age will severely alter its appearance. I like to believe it was the artist's intention to knowingly create another picture of Dorian Gray and watch with fascination as changes in the perishable pigments of the pressed flowers faded, changed to rust, or bleached away, altering the features in a most dramatic way.

Any time pressed-flower pictures are displayed, lighting must come under consideration. Fluorescent lights do not flatter the soft, muted tones of pressed flowers. They also emit rays similar to sunshine that cause the flowers to fade at a greatly accelerated rate. If electric outlets are available at a show, you might consider supplying your own lamps with incandescent lights.

If your designs are shown out of doors, the pictures should be displayed in a roofed area or hung so that they face north, out of the direct rays of the sun. Sun will accelerate the aging of the natural colors of pressed flowers, and, though felt-pen ink used to dye the flowers is labelled "permanent," it is dramatically perishable when exposed to the sun. After eight hours in direct sun, all the felt-pen ink color on the flowers will have disappeared.

To begin a design, spread your collection of pressed materials out on a large table so they are visually available as you work. This will allow you to make choices quickly without stopping to dig through boxes of pressed materials. At first, it might be a good idea to practise combining the various flowers and leaves together right out on the table without any thought to framing the outcome. This will allow your natural creative instincts to flow freely. Working within the confined area of a frame or with a preconceived idea of style can restrict the growth of your design.

For inspiration, for ideas, or for outright copying, study books on flower arranging, floral upholstery and drapery designs, stitchery, wallpaper patterns, and decorations on commercially packaged products. Observe the natural growth of flowers, leaves, stems, and buds and imitate the lines seen in nature. Notice the way a stem bends from the weight of a heavy flower or how the lower flowers on a stalk open while buds at the top are still green and undeveloped. Leaves develop in the same way—those at the tip of a spray opening last. One of the added benefits of a hobby such as this is a renewed appreciation for the beauty of nature and its infinite variety of shapes and colors. Trees, shrubs, and plants that went unnoticed for years will suddenly reveal themselves in the spectacular color of their foliage, the unusual grace of a stem lifting its flower up to drink in the sun, or in the intricate way that a flower's petals join together.

The flowers, leaves, stems, and buds that you gather should be used in a natural way. A flower that projects beyond another flower should be visibly supported by a stem that can be traced between the mass of flowers. Vine tendrils and buds should be placed so as to emulate believable natural growth habits. The viewer's eye should not trip over careless additions that have little relationship to the rest of the arrangement.

Start with a small, but not tiny, frame. Miniatures under 4″ × 5″ can present difficulties. Working with tiny plant materials can exhaust a beginner's patience before the design has been

Illus. 9-2. When creating a pressed-flower picture, spread out your supply of plant materials so that they are close at hand. Study the natural shapes and growth patterns of flowers and leaves so that you can recreate them in your designs.

completed, and flowers that are too large often appear crowded and ready to burst out of a little frame. An 8″ × 10″ frame is a nice size for a beginner. Oval frames of this size lend themselves particularly well to pressed-flower designs. Rectangular frames can present problems because their corners have a tendency to end up as empty dead space. When choosing a frame, keep in mind the depth of the opening. It must be deep enough to hold the glass, the rigid backboard, and the polyester fibrefill padding. Before buying frames, see the detailed instructions given for selecting and outfitting a frame in Chapter 8.

After the frame has been fitted out with glass, a rigid backboard, and a back cover, it is time to select a proper background fabric. When selecting fabric colors, take a few of the flowers to the store and hold them against the different fabric in natural light. Fluorescent lights do not flatter pressed-flower colors and they mask the true col-

ors of fabrics. Select a color that does not overpower the muted colors of the pressed flowers. They will appear drab in contrast with brightly dyed fabrics. Red flowers will seem more vivid when shown against an ivory or pale yellow background. Be aware of the impact the background color will make on a design. It is as much a part of the color scheme as the flowers themselves.

The colors used in an arrangement should support the style, line, and motion of the design. Strong colors work best with strong, bold lines, whereas soft colors enhance a soft, gentle design. The background should always be thought of as one of the colors in a design. As it shows up between the flowers and throughout the design, it will become part of the pattern. Judge the background's impact on the total effect as you place the flowers against it by alternately covering it over with vegetation or allowing it to show. Use the same care in exposing the background as you do in distributing the various colored flowers.

A neutral background of off-white assimilates the greatest number of colors and does not dominate a design. Very dark backgrounds, such as black, dark brown, navy blue, or forest green, are also neutral colors. They can almost be considered no background at all. Seldom interfering with a color scheme, they outline shape, form, and line so that the flowers stand out prominently, especially when lighter colored flowers dominate the design.

Cut the fabric you have selected so that it is the same size as the glass that fits inside the frame. Set the frame, padding, rigid backboard, and back cover aside. Place the fabric, right side up, on top of the glass. The entire arrangement will be worked with the glass under the fabric. Use tweezers to handle the flowers. To grasp a flower with the tweezers, slide the tweezers under one end of the flower while gently pressing on the opposite side of the flower, causing it to rise slightly on the tweezers' side. Although others recommend a needle or small watercolor brush for nudging pressed flowers into position, I do not think that they give the proper kind of control. I merely mention them here for those who might find that those tools work well for them.

The design possibilities of pressed-flower pictures are limited only by the imagination, provided the design is allowed to evolve unobstructed by flowers that are glued to one spot. No sooner is a flower placed "just so" than you will want to shift, remove, or replace it. The position of each flower, leaf, bud, or tendril will be dependent upon its relationship to all the other flowers and leaves surrounding it. As flowers are added and the design grows, this relationship constantly changes. Until the arrangement is ready for framing, adjustments will take place.

Flowers should not be used simply to fill space in the corners of the frame. As the eye follows the motion that runs through the arrangement, strong lines throughout the design give life and vitality to the flowers. The lines of your design should be carried out in a subtle way. They should be more than a succession of flowers placed end to end in soldierly fashion.

You may create lines through the design that occasionally cross or join together to add variety, but they should never affect the basic theme of the design. Let your eye constantly follow the lines that develop in the design to check for continuity. In a massed arrangement, this is particularly important. For example, in a triangular arrangement, lines running throughout will make the difference between a design and a hodgepodge pyramid of flowers.

An arrangement that mimics a growing plant should have stems that meet at the base, appearing to share a common root system. Begin with sprays and then gradually add leaves and buds to them. When adding stems, push the blunt ends behind a leaf, stem, or bud so that they appear to be growing out of a natural source. Many times the direction a spray takes does not quite fit into the lines of a design. In this case, simply break the bud, flower, or leaf off its original stem and pair it with stems that have lines more complementary to the design.

The undergrowth in a pressed-flower picture must be kept to a minimum. Undergrowth is the accumulation of stems, leaves, or sprays of baby's breath crisscrossing underneath the flowers. Large sprays should not be laid down on the background and then covered over with flowers. In time, this undergrowth will cause wrinkles and creases on the delicate petals of the flowers as they conform to the shape of the stems running beneath them. To simulate the effect of a spray or stem running behind the arrangement, the parts of the spray that are under the flowers should be broken away, leaving only the beginning and end of the spray protruding beyond the flower. Be sure to align the stem where it enters and leaves the design for an appearance of continuity.

Center of Gravity

It is important that a center of gravity be evident so that the flowers appear to be connected at some central point. They should not seem to float around lost in space. Both leaves and flowers contribute to the perspective in a design. Plant materials that emanate from the center of gravity and face towards the outer edges of the design can help establish a cohesive whole. Pointed leaves have a bit of an advantage over rounded leaves because they can be used to indicate movement and enhance direction, drawing the eye through the lines of an arrangement.

In order to create the center of gravity in a narrow, vertical spray, the flowers and leaves above the center should face upwards and away from the center and the flowers below the center should face downwards (Illus. 9–3). Flowers in the center of the spray should face towards the left and right.

When making a triangular arrangement, it helps to imagine the flowers in a vase. All the flowers must be placed in a way that strengthens this image. If a flower is placed vertically on the far left or far right of such an arrangement, it would be at odds with the vase image.

Artificial Enhancement

Seldom will a spray of flowers or leaves just happen to fall in place perfectly with the lines in an arrangement. As a result, the individual ingredients of pressed-plant design must often be manipulated to suit the situation. A spray of leaves or flowers can be built up by placing large leaves or flowers at the lowest point on the stem, increasingly smaller leaves or flowers towards the end, and tiny leaves or buds at the tips. If the flowers and leaves are closely aligned, a stem may not be necessary. However, if a stem is required, arrange the leaves or flowers so that they appear to be attached to the stem in a natural manner.

Folded leaves often add a nice dimension of perspective to a picture. If all the leaves are left full face, a stiff stilted effect will permeate the design. If folded leaves are not available, you can cut the leaves into curved halves with a curved cutting tool to give an effect that is similar to folded leaves. Fern that are constantly repeated in an "A" shape can become repetitive. For variety, cut a few in half lengthwise every now and then.

Illus. 9-3. This arrangement of Queen Anne's lace, rose geranium, and wild radish exhibits a strong center of gravity at the point where the vase (fashioned from the stems of grass) and the flowers meet. This effect was created by placing the flowers in a circular pattern that faces out from the center.

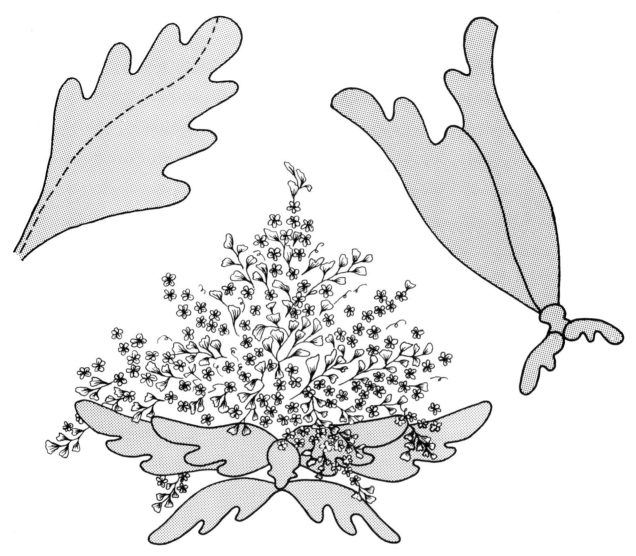

Illus. 9-4. If you can't seem to find the right flower, you can take several flowers apart, cut them into different shapes, and rearrange them to form contrived flowers. Here, dusty miller leaves (top right) have been cut in curved halves and reassembled to form a tall vase (top left) and a compote (center).

It is not often that the perfect bud, leaf, stem, or flower is available for a particular spot in a design. Be inventive and you can usually manipulate the materials on hand in whatever way that strikes your fancy. A single petal from a flower can be cut down and used to create a bud. Then you can slip it under the end of a tiny leaf spray. Dimension and depth can be enhanced in a flower that has been pressed in profile by slipping a loose petal behind the profiled petals, allowing it to protrude slightly. Stamens from another flower can also be inserted between the petals for perspective, making a new, contrived flower.

The perspective of individual blossoms carries over into the total effect, adding life and movement to the inert materials. Some of the flowers should appear to be in back of others, standing straight and tall and others should appear to be turning away or nodding. This will avoid the monotony caused by flowers that are all displayed full face.

Some flowers, such as geranium florets, splay

open when pressed full face, leaving large open spaces at the center of the flower. This unattractive effect can be corrected by covering the area with stamens from another flower.

The petals from two lobelias can be manipulated to form a six-petalled flower. Flowers whose petals have wide spaces between them, such as pearblossoms, can be coupled with another of its kind, and, by offsetting the petals, one flower can fill in spaces left by the other.

Botanical Studies

The flower press played an important role in days of herbal medicine, when the science of botany was closely associated with the science of medicine. A good collection of pressed plant materials was invaluable to botanists engaged in the identification, classification, and study of the new and unusual plants that world explorers regularly brought back from distant lands.

Early books on botany were illustrated with detailed drawings of plants. A single plant or flower was shown in the various aspects of its growth: root structure, stem, foliation, bud, flower, and seeding process. These botanical studies make equally interesting subjects for pressed-flower pictures, in which all or only a few of the factors can be used.

Color

It is not a formidable task to select colors for a pressed-flower picture, and you may feel that an analytical approach takes all the fun out of it. However, there will be times when a design fights back and a vague feeling persists that it "needs something." Instead of just hoping to fall upon a cure, a critical review of color might lead you to a solution. You must, however, keep in mind the basic elements of color and design.

The color wheel (Illus. 9–5), which displays the names of the color hues, is a reference used by artists to determine the natural blending of hues. Opposites on the color wheel, such as blue and orange or violet and yellow, are complementary

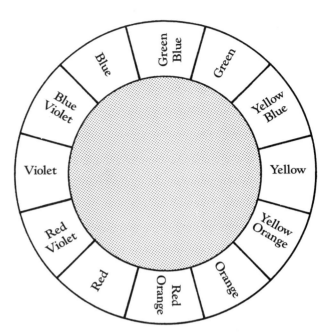

Illus. 9-5. The color wheel is a useful reference for the pressed-flower arranger because it provides quick guidance for the most attractive color combinations.

harmonies. These sharp contrasts of color are full of energy and spirit and give strength and vigor to bold lines. When complementary hues produce an effect that seems harsh, they can be softened by adding close relatives (analogous harmonies) of the colors you are using. These can be found on the spectrum on each side of your basic colors.

The easy gradations of analogous harmonies (yellow, yellow orange, orange, red orange, red) can produce gentle, soft effects. However, if an analogous harmony develops from gentle and soft to tame and weak, the contrast of a complementary hue from the opposite side of the wheel (blue) will pep up the design.

Two primary colors can be made more harmonious by adding a shared color or the color they would make if mixed together. For example, an arrangement of red and yellow flowers can be harmonized by the addition of orange flowers, because the red and yellow, when mixed, make orange. You can also balance the design by choosing one flower with a particular color in its middle and another flower with the same color on the edges of its petals. You can always add sharpness and character to a lifeless arrangement with the addition of a few white flowers.

Most often we design pressed-flower pictures to blend in with a particular color scheme in a home. However, designing a picture that is an end in itself affords a more creative atmosphere for developing your own unique style. But keep in mind that some color combinations might be difficult to assimilate into a home decor, such as orange, purple, and lavender on a bright yellow background. Although off-white could have been used here for a background, the colors will always look better against a yellow background and only so-so against off-white.

The amount of each color to use is also an important thing to consider. The strength of the primary colors in the flowers and the background, as well as the size of your design will determine color amounts. Colors should be used in unequal quantities, but one should always be dominant. You should not have any isolated blocks of color that stand alone. It is impossible to say "use so much of this or so much of that" because each person has a different conception of color and no two people see color in the same way.

It is important to understand the color wheel and its complementary and analogous harmonies, but some properties of color do not apply to this craft. Minute gradations, such as blue violet/violet blue, or turquoise/blue green, will seldom be a part of your stock of pressed flowers. Though you may use felt-pen ink for vibrant colors and chalk for softer tones, highly refined abstractions of each color, such as those found in a paint box or in live flowers, do not exist in pressed flowers. Although the color wheel shows green to be complementary to red, the maroon or burgundy color of dried red roses combined with the dull color of most pressed green leaves does not give strength and vigor to a design. In fact, it often gives the design a rather gloomy appearance. Moreover, the green leaves will lose their green coloring after one year's exposure to light.

Although greens are rarely the dominant color in a live bouquet, they are of great importance to a pressed-flower picture. Leaves should be distributed through the design with as much care

and thought as the flowers. Bright green leaves, such as maidenhair fern, seem to contrast sharply with pressed flower colors no matter where their color is found on the wheel. After these leaves have aged to a softer, more neutral color, they blend with the soft, muted colors of pressed flowers. This factor must be kept in mind when choosing the ingredients of a design. The green leaves must be an asset in a freshly completed arrangement as well as its aged counterpart.

Vivid colors in a background can dominate the color scheme of an arrangement, making a balance difficult to achieve. The color not only surrounds the entire arrangement but shows in patches between the flowers and leaves. Colors that might harmonize well across from each other can suffer if the background is constantly appearing and reappearing among them. If a design seems to be at a standstill, check the colors. Has the design developed in such a way that the flowers have outgrown your original choice of background color? Is it simply a case of a good design on an ill-conceived background?

After assembling all the flowers for an arrangement, the enthusiasm of the moment must be curbed while you are dyeing certain flowers whose colors will not hold up. Dyeing the flowers with felt-pen ink can be time-consuming and repetitive. Perishable yellow flowers must be dyed yellow and perishable orange flowers dyed orange. Pastel-colored flowers, if not treated with chalk when they were pressed, should be touched up with chalk for greater durability. If the aging process of an important flower in an arrangement is unknown, it should not be used until one of its kind has been tested on a sunny windowsill for two months. If, at the end of that time, the color has bleached away or there has been considerable fading, artificial color should be added. If the flower turns rust red, a decision must be made to ascertain this discoloration's impact on the color scheme after it has aged. No design of merit should contain flowers that have not been tested and then treated for improved durability when their color has been found to be perishable.

A competent artisan, one who has taken the time to test the durability of the flowers and leaves and who understands the character of each flower used in a picture, will visualize the changed appearance and know what to expect as the flowers age. This expertise will be evident after the picture has aged because a picture that ages well is no accident. When durable, harmonious color, whether natural or treated, is present, a few perishable flowers in the arrangement can add charm. Good design survives both lives—the new and the old.

In one design that I made, the brown color of aged red roses added a patina. The original arrangement consisted of pastel blooms and wild red roses resting in a vase contrived of white dusty miller leaves that were trimmed for effect. The piece was framed in brown. The dusty miller and the pastel flowers did not change color, but the red roses discolored to brown. The brown frame exactly repeated the color in the aged roses, making them an asset to the total effect. In long-range planning, an experienced designer incorpo-rates a blend of flowers, frame, liner, and back-ground color into the original design to enhance the flowers in both the original and the aged design.

The Crescent

A crescent design lends itself well to pressed-flower pictures because the design follows the curve of an oval frame (Illus. 9–6). Always allow a small margin of empty space near the frame. Flowers and leaves should not be arranged right up to the edge or appear crowded into their allotted space. Hold the frame over your work now and then, checking to see that the arrangement has not become lopsided or moved too close to the edge. When adding to an arrangement (Illus. 9–7), push the blunt end of a new stem down

Illus. 9-6 (left) and 9-7 (right). The crescent design is a good choice for a beginner. Here, the arrange-ment has been started with a few sprigs of heather, which form the outline. Next, the shape is more clearly defined and flowers are added.

Illus. 9-8 (left) and 9-9 (right). Small sprigs of heather are added to the crescent as finishing touches and the design is completed with the addition of vine tendrils.

behind other pressed plant materials so that it will appear to be attached to the rest of the arrangement.

The design can be embellished (Illus. 9–8) as much as you wish with various flowers, leaves, fern, and tendrils, so long as the basic crescent line is still visible. The center of gravity in a crescent design should always be in the bowl at the bottom of the arch, with related elements in the arrangement reaching out beyond that point.

After an arrangement has been completed (Illus. 9–9), check to see if any vegetation has shifted or any blunt stubby ends have popped out. Carefully push them back into position. Clean up any bits of debris or dust that may have fallen on the background by either brushing them away with a soft watercolor brush or gently picking them up with the moistened end of a tweezer. You can then consider the design complete and ready to slide off the glass, down onto the padded surface, and into the frame.

If some of the vegetation has shifted after the glass is already in place, it can still be corrected before the work is framed. Hold the glass down on the flowers with a very light touch while sliding a thin knife or screwdriver under the glass. Aim right for the piece of vegetation that needs to be nudged back into position. With a little practice, you will be able to press the screwdriver down lightly against the padded surface, slide it under the outlying vegetation, and reach flowers or buds in the middle of the arrangement. If the arrangement is properly transferred to the padded surface in preparation for framing, such adjustments should not often be necessary. Be sure the implement does not have rough edges or nicks that might catch on the fabric. The blunt end of a very thin screwdriver is sometimes better to use than a knife because the thin point of the knife tends to slide right past the offending bud or stem. Withdraw the tool with a slight downward pressure against the padded surface so that you do not disturb other parts of the arrangement.

Nosegay

Another arrangement of pressed flowers that is easy for beginners is a nosegay of flowers. The center of gravity in a nosegay is at the base of the bouquet where the flowers all appear to be fastened together, with the stems trailing below. Stems inserted below the flowers should line up with some of the flowers above so that they appear to be supporting the flowers. Use two curved stems that crisscross each other and add one or two straight stems for variety. Or use four or five stick-straight stems arranged in perfect unison.

Wreath or Circle of Flowers

A wreath design is very effective and easy to make. All you need is a good selection of flowers in a variety of colors and in graded sizes ranging from 1½″ maximum, to ¾″, ½″, ¼″, and so on, down to tiny wisps of grass, vine tendrils, buds, small leaves, and fern.

For a beginner, an 11″ × 14″ oval would be the easiest to manage for this design. If a smaller frame is used, the largest flowers should be only 1″ in diameter. Though an 8″ × 10″ frame could accommodate a wreath, the space available for a little nosegay in the middle would be limited.

Start with four or five of the largest flowers and distribute them unevenly around the oval (Illus. 9–10). Also lay one down in the middle for the nosegay.

Then distribute about nine or ten of the next smaller flowers unevenly around the oval, and again place one in the center for the nosegay. Do not start to arrange the nosegay until the full selection of flowers has been accumulated there.

Continue distributing flowers of smaller and smaller size around the circle of flowers. As the circle begins to fill, start to arrange them by nudging them closer together, tucking some partly under others, extending some out of the outer or inner edges of the circle, and adding a

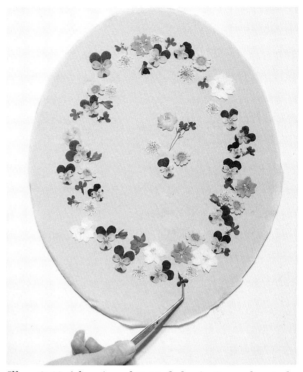

Illus. 9-10 (above) and 9-11 (below). Start the circle of flowers by dividing your pressed materials into size categories. Then, arrange them in the circle, starting with the largest and ending with the smallest. Each time you add a size group to the outer ring, add a flower of that size to the center for a nosegay.

Illus. 9-12. Because there will be more small flowers in the wreath, make sure that you vary the style and color to avoid repetition.

selection of tiny leaves, buds, and fern between the flowers (Illus. 9–11). Use pieces of fern from the tips of a frond because these are the smallest. Cut leaves and fern in half lengthwise and/or use leaves that have been folded so that they appear to be nodding around the edge of the wreath.

Because there will be very many small flowers, several different types and colors will be more effective and help to avoid repetition in the design. The larger flowers can be very much alike because there will be so few of them.

When all the flowers and leaves have been arranged, add tiny wisps of grass and vine tendrils around the inner and outer edges of the circle for an interesting embellishment.

Last, arrange the nosegay of flowers in the center of the circle, either with or without stems below it (Illus. 9–12).

"S" Curve

This design begins with two flowers placed in the center of the picture. If the flowers are placed at an angle, rather than on a lateral or horizontal plane, they will be more pleasing to the eye. A gracefully curved spray of grass that has gone to seed should be inserted in the hollow where the two flowers meet, forming the top half of the "S" curve. The blunt end of the spray should be hidden under the petals of the flowers. Insert a second spray of grass below to form the lower half of the curve (Illus. 9–13a).

The center of gravity in this design is located between the two large flowers in the middle of the arrangement. Therefore, subsequent elements of the design should emanate from that point. The two sprays of grass project out from this center of gravity. The base of all the leaves in the arrangement should face this point (Illus. 9–13b) so that their tips direct the eye away from the center of gravity. This will give movement and life to the design.

The basic design can be embellished with any number of leaves, flowers, fern, or tendrils so long as the "S"-curve line is still visible (Illus. 9–14).

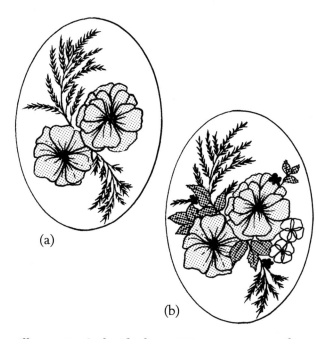

(a)

(b)

Illus. 9-13a & b. The basic "S" curve consists of two flowers and two sprays of foliage (a). When other plant materials are added, they must radiate outward from the center along the lines of the "S" shape (b).

Illus. 9-14. As long as the basic "S" shape is maintained, you may embellish this type of arrangement as much as you like.

Advanced Designing

When a designer has advanced to larger arrangements, the style, color, size, and shape of a piece will take precedence over the framing. In other words, the design will be conceived outside the confining spatial and stylistic limitations of a frame (Illus. 9–15).

At this stage, the background fabric must be cut to an ample size and laid out on a large piece of cardboard. Unrestricted designs may grow to three or four feet, or may never develop beyond 16″ × 20″. But if the background fabric is cut too small and the design develops beyond the size of the fabric, the design cannot be transferred from one background to another without throwing it all out of kilter.

When size appears to be well established, a frame can be chosen to enhance the arrangement. In choosing a frame, consider the subject as well as the color, selecting something that complements the color of the design without overpowering its subject. There are frames of many styles: country, oriental, lacquer, art deco, silver and gold metallic, 18th Century, or French provincial. There are round, oval, square, rectangular, and even fan-shaped frames available. You may also add a mat, which can sometimes enhance the setting by repeating one of the colors in the arrangement. If the design does not fit standard-sized frames (which very often happens), you must have one custom made at a frame shop.

If the piece is quite large, it will be inconvenient to clamp the unframed picture together to take to the frame shop. In this case, make up a little unframed sampler consisting of the background fabric and one or two of each of the flowers and greenery used in the design. With this sampler in hand, you can easily judge the effect of various colors and styles of frames and mats against the colors in the arrangement.

After the frame has been selected and a piece of glass has been cut to fit it, carefully center the glass on top of the arrangement and mark the perimeter on the background fabric. Remove the glass (do this very carefully so that the pressed materials are not disturbed) and cut the fabric along the line. Slide the glass under the fabric, and discard the original cardboard that was under it.

If you are framing a completed design that is three or more feet long, you will need the assistance of another person. One of you must hold on to the fabric while the other pulls the glass away, allowing the design to drop safely onto the polyester fibrefill pad. Turning a large piece upside down also requires some dexterity and cooperation with another person. The glass and frame must be held firmly pressed against the design to prevent any of the plant materials from shifting out of place.

Signing Your Work

In order to sign your work, you can purchase a stylus at a glass shop or a hobby shop. This will allow you to etch your name on the front of the glass. Or, you can imprint your name on the inside of the glass with a rubber stamp of your signature in reverse. However, ordinary stamp pad ink cannot be used on glass. A heavy paint-like ink must be used instead. This can be purchased where rubber stamps are made.

Illus. 9-15. Once you have gained some experience in pressed-flower arranging, your designs can grow and evolve with your imagination. You will no longer need to arrange within the confines of a basic frame shape. For example, this design was arranged on a large piece of fabric and later mounted in a custom-made frame.

Photographing Your Work

I have always found it necessary to photograph each of my pictures. First of all, I could never let go of the darned things and sell them without feeling a sense of loss. Second (after I got over the sale), the photographs became a record of how I handled certain problems in preserving various styles of wedding bouquets.

Photographs can be useful in assessing your own progress. I found it useful to review photographs of my work from year to year. Photographs of my early work show that they were very sparsely filled because I was afraid of losing the line of an arrangement. I also made notes beside pictures that sold, such as when and where it was displayed and how quickly it sold. If a design sold well, I repeated it over and over again. I found that the public was most attracted to designs that had lots and lots of flowers in them.

Photographs taken with a flash can sometimes result in a photo of the flash reflected in the glass. I prefer to photograph my work outside in the sun, but there, you must watch for reflections of trees and telephone wires. In either case, tilt the picture so that the camera is not aimed at a perfect right angle, or stand off to one side of the picture to angle the shot.

Repeating or Copying Designs

It is possible to repeat a design by making a paper pattern of it. Fit a piece of thin tracing paper over the glass that covers the picture and tape it in place with masking tape. Trace over the flowers, making an outline of each of the flowers in the arrangement. Use colored pencils if it is necessary to distinguish between flowers of similar size and shape. Remove the paper and punch a hole directly in the middle of each of the outlined flowers.

To use the pattern, cut a piece of background fabric for the new picture and center the paper pattern on the cloth. (There will be a margin of cloth uncovered by the pattern where the lip of the frame is located.) Mix very small amounts of several colors of powdered tempera chalk with water. Through the holes that have been punched in the paper pattern, apply a small spot of the tempera paint on the background fabric, using a different color tempera paint for each variety of flower in the design.

Remove the paper pattern and place the appropriate flowers on the dots of paint. It is not necessary to mark the location of leaves. Leaves can be inserted after the flowers are all in place, following the drawing on the tracing paper.

10

Designing a Shoji

One of the most interesting projects for the pressed-flower artist is a rice-paper screen, or a shoji. With pressed flowers embedded between its sheets of rice paper, the shoji creates a conversation piece that is a beautiful and unusual addition to a room. I would recommend some practice making small samplers of flowers embedded in rice paper before embarking on such an ambitious project as a shoji.

Materials

The screen can be ordered custom-made through a professional decorator. Screens are equipped with wood inserts in the back of each panel that are easily removed to install the flowers.

Rice paper is available where art supplies are sold. The weight and style of the paper varies considerably from shipment to shipment because the paper is made by hand.

Two types of rice paper are needed for a shoji: a plain type for the back of the panel, and a type with silk threads scattered throughout it. This type will be used as the front of the panel of flowers. Both papers should be of as thin a grade as possible so that the flowers can be seen.

You will need to experiment a bit with samples of rice paper to determine which are sheer enough to allow the flowers to be seen. Glue greatly enhances the visibility of the flowers after it has dried.

Aluminum foil is used with each sheet of rice paper while work is in progress.

Cardboard stretchers must be made, one for each panel of rice paper in the screen, to prevent them from shrinking and puckering as they dry.

White glue will be mixed with equal parts of water to be used all over the rice paper panel. A very small amount of tacky glue will be needed to keep the flowers from shifting about during construction.

Brushes: One soft 3″ brush, as well as a few small- and medium-sized soft watercolor brushes.

A stapler, utility knife, ruler, and of course the ever present **tweezers** to handle the flowers.

Flowers should be thin with durable color or have color added with felt-pen ink.

Chalk cannot be used to color flowers that are embedded in rice paper, and the usually durable color of forget-me-nots can turn brown when white glue is applied to these flowers. When glue is undiluted or mixed in stronger proportion, it will cause many flowers to show discoloration after the glue has dried.

Construction

To complete this project, you will need a fairly large work area. Your work space should be in a

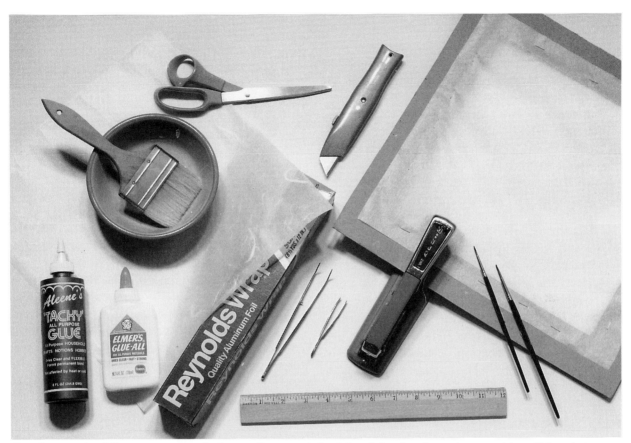

Illus. 10–1. The following appear clockwise, from top left. A bowl for the glue mixture with a 3″ brush is used to apply the glue all over the sheet of rice paper. The scissors are for cutting the rice paper. A utility knife in safety handle is needed to cut stretcher frames out of cardboard. Next is a small sample of a stretcher with a plain sheet of rice paper attached. (The flowers are arranged on this sheet.) Small brushes are used to apply glue to the flowers. A stapler should be available to attach the rice paper to the stretchers, a ruler to center the design on each panel, and a tweezers to handle the flowers. Aluminum foil is used during construction. Diluted white glue is used to bond the two sheets of rice paper together, and a small amount of tacky glue is needed to hold the flowers in place during construction. Under the bowl is the type of rice paper with silk threads running through it. This is the paper that will cover the front of the flower arrangement.

part of the house where it will not interfere with daily household activities because the project will take several weeks to complete.

MAKING THE STRETCHERS

To construct the cardboard stretchers for the rice paper panels, remove the wood frame inserts from the back of the screen. Then center each insert on top of pieces of cardboard that are approximately 2″ larger than the inserts. Trace an outline around the outside of the insert.

Remove the wood insert and, with a utility knife, cut an opening in the cardboard along the traced line, creating a frame of cardboard. Make one stretcher for each panel in the screen.

PREPARING RICE PAPER

Cut a piece of rice paper, a little larger than the stretcher opening, for each stretcher. At the same time, cut the same number of pieces of the rice paper with silk threads and set aside for later use. Staple each sheet of plain rice paper onto the edges of a stretcher, making sure that it is straight, taut, and wrinkle free.

PREPARING ALUMINUM FOIL

Cut pieces of aluminum foil that are twice as many as the panels in the screen. They should be the same size as the stretchers. Set half the pieces aside.

Lay the sheets of the aluminum foil on the workbench and place on top each of the stretchers and rice paper. Do not staple the foil to the stretchers.

ARRANGING FLOWERS

Make a flower arrangement on each of the rice paper panels. Avoid placing flowers at the very edge of the panels. A small margin of empty space must be allowed along the edge for mounting the panel in the shoji frame. Plan and arrange a design for each of the panels before proceeding with glue so that there is some correlation between the arrangements in each of the various panels. Use a ruler, when necessary, to center your design.

GLUING FLOWERS

When all of the designs have been completed to your satisfaction, you must glue each piece of vegetation in place with very small spots of tacky glue—just enough to keep the flowers from shifting out of position when the rice paper is laid over them.

Apply glue with the small watercolor brushes, so that you can reach whatever part of the flower is most readily available without disturbing its position. Do not use white glue mixture for this step because it does not adhere until it is dry.

Care must be taken during this process to prevent the rice paper from sticking to the aluminum foil below. Each time glue is applied to a piece of vegetation, you must slide a sheet of paper under the panel (between the panel and the aluminum foil) to break contact between the foil and the rice paper.

Once you have glued all the flowers to the bases of the panels, you will be ready to glue on the top layers of the rice paper.

Note: From this point on, work on only one panel at a time. Complete all the remaining steps without interruption.

Have ready:

A bowl of glue mixture
Small watercolor brushes and 3″ brush
One of the extra sheets of aluminum foil
One of the pieces of rice paper with silk
   threads.

Aluminum Foil →

Rice Paper ⟶

Aluminum Foil →

Illus. 10-2. When you are ready to join the two sheets of rice paper, use the aluminum foil to handle the glue-soaked upper sheet. It simply is peeled off once the rice paper pieces are aligned and firmly pressed together.

Using a soft watercolor brush, apply the white glue mixture between the petals of all the multi-petalled flowers.

Next apply white glue on the top surface of each of the larger flowers and leaves. (Glue need not be applied over the tops of smaller flowers, leaves, buds, or stems.) The glue will bead up on top of the vegetation. It is not possible to apply the glue evenly over the surface of the flowers and leaves.

Note: The glue on top of the flowers must not be allowed to harden before the next step is completed.

Immediately after the glue has been applied to the top surface of the flowers in the arrangement, the second sheet of rice paper must be prepared and laid over the top of the flower arrangement.

Lay the sheet of rice paper on top of the sheet of aluminum foil that was cut earlier and brush the glue mixture all over the surface of the paper. The paper will readily absorb the glue. Do not brush the surface of the paper over and over because it might weaken and tear. It should be wet all over but not dripping wet. The paper will at this point adhere to the aluminum foil.

Before you cover the flowers, decide whether you will need another pair of hands to help hold the paper straight as you line up the edges of the two sheets.

Then pick up the rice paper and attached aluminum foil. Turn the sheets over so that the aluminum foil is on the top and the rice paper underneath (Illus. 10–2). Lay the rice paper down on top of the flower arrangement, making sure that the edges of the paper match.

Reminder: The sheet of aluminum foil should still be under the panel of rice paper that bears the flowers.

At this point the layers should be in the following order: a sheet of aluminum foil, the stretcher with the plain rice paper and flowers, the rice paper wet with glue, and, on top, the second sheet of aluminum foil.

Press down firmly against the aluminum foil to affix the rice paper with silk threads onto the rice paper that is stapled to the stretcher.

Gently peel off the sheet of aluminum foil on

Illus. 10-3. A shoji is a unique way to display a pressed flower arrangement because the rice paper allows light to shine through the design.

the top, taking care that you are not removing the rice paper with it.

If some areas of the panel do not appear to be firmly affixed, dab up and down against those areas with a dry brush. Generally speaking, additional glue will not be needed, but if areas over

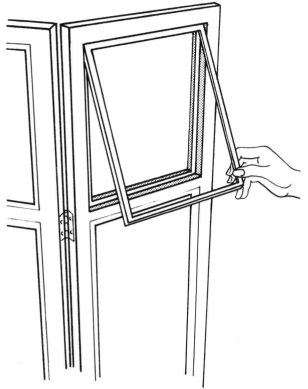

Illus. 10-4. In order to mount the rice paper panel, simply remove the wooden frame, push the rice paper panel into the screen, and replace the frame.

large flowers and leaves appear dry, then add a very small amount of glue and dab up and down on those areas to work the glue down through the paper and onto the leaves or flowers.

DRYING THE PANEL

Lift the stretcher off the workbench and turn it upside down on a clean work area. Remove the aluminum foil from the back of the panel.

Allow the panel to dry standing up on its side for a short while (about 10 minutes). After this short drying period, lay the stretcher down on a flat clean surface and weigh it down on the sides with books or other heavy objects to prevent it from warping. Lift the panel from time to time to make sure that it is not adhering to the workbench.

After the panel has thoroughly dried, cut it away from the stretcher with a utility knife, following along the edge of the stretcher window.

IRONING THE PANEL

Using low heat, iron the panel of flowers between two sheets of wax paper. A hard, flat surface padded with several layers of bed sheets makes a better surface for ironing the panels than does an ironing board.

MOUNTING THE PANELS

Remove the wooden insert from the back of the shoji (Illus. 10–4) and glue the panel to the inside edge of the insert. Install the insert in the shoji by placing a bit of glue in each corner.

Displaying the Shoji Screen

Do not display the screen where it will be exposed to direct sun or fluorescent light. An incandescent light behind the screen will show the flowers to best advantage and cause the least amount of fading. To prevent drying, rub Armor All™ (or a similar plastic protectant) on rice paper panels once a year or more often if necessary.

11

Pressing and Preserving Wedding Bouquets

Only someone reasonably proficient in the craft, who has successfully pressed, arranged, and framed larger pressed-flower pictures, should attempt to preserve wedding bouquets. This chapter contains five examples of wedding bouquets, including photographs of each bouquet as it is being assembled and readied for framing.

Reproducing the Style of a Bouquet

After a wedding bouquet has been transformed into its new one-dimensional form, it should be as accurate a representation of the original bouquet as possible. If the live bouquet was a pear-shaped cascade with flowers packed tightly together, that is the form it should take when it is dried, reassembled, and framed. Nosegays can be anywhere from 10″ to 15″ in diameter. The number of flowers in any given bouquet varies to a considerable degree. Three dozen flowers can make up a small 12″ nosegay, whereas two dozen flowers might be used for a cascade 28″ long. All the characteristics that make a bouquet unique must be observed if it is to be reassembled accurately.

The only exceptions to the rule of accuracy are the bouquet's hardware and plastic flowers. Items such as pearl corsage pins used in the throats of stephanotis or pearl hearts or butterflies used among the live flowers cannot be arranged in the pressed version of the bouquet. Such hard pieces of decoration would crush the delicate pressed materials, as would stiff bulky plastic flowers.

The size, style, and content of a bouquet should be carefully noted when the bouquet is received for preservation. Measure both the width and the length of the bouquet with a ruler. Count all the flowers. Also make notes on the style of the bouquet.

A photograph of the bouquet is seldom clear enough to use as a reference for placement of the flowers. Sketches and notes describing the details of a bouquet are far better guides. A few lines quickly drawn to represent the various flowers will show location in the bouquet. Use abbreviations to indicate the different types of undergrowth—BB for baby's breath, LL for leatherleaf fern, MH for maidenhair fern, and so on.

Florists often decorate bouquets by tucking bows and tufts of net among the flowers. Bows can be represented by arched lines where they are located in the bouquet. A few crosshatched lines can represent net. A few lines will indicate ribbon streamers and a wiggly line around a sketch can pinpoint the position of a doily.

Receiving a Bouquet

The bride should have her flowers delivered to you on the day of the wedding. The flowers should not be held over until the next day or stored at home in a refrigerator, which is too cold for storing flowers for more than an hour or two. The delicate petals of roses are easily frostbitten if kept at a very low temperature. If leaves are not covered with a plastic bag they will dry out considerably in a home refrigerator.

Flowers, if tightly closed in a plastic bag on a hot summer day, will suffocate and become limp. Flowers should not be covered with plastic unless they are refrigerated.

In cold weather, brides should be cautioned to protect the flowers while outdoors. The tips of flower petals can very quickly be nipped by frost when temperatures are below 0 °F and will discolor when they are dried.

Dismantling a Bouquet

After the bride's flowers have been received, the bouquet has been measured, the flowers counted, and a sketch and notes have been made about the characteristics of the bouquet, it can be dismantled.

In some bouquets, the flower stems are simply inserted in an oasis or in styrofoam. These bouquets are easy to dismantle.

In other bouquets, however, the stems are removed and the flowers are attached to wire stems (Illus. 11–1). Large cascades are almost always firmly wired.

Roses are usually wired through the calyx. Using a wire cutter, cut the wires right below the calyx and straighten them. Firmly grasp each wire with a narrow long-nosed pliers and pull it straight out without tearing the calyx.

Mum daisies are wired with a loop pushed down through the top of the flower. Cut the wire below the flower and, with a long-nosed pliers,

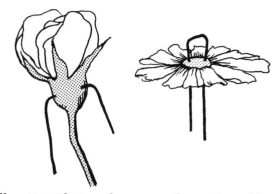

Illus. 11-1. Florists often mount flowers in wedding bouquets using wire. Roses are usually wired through the calyx and daisies through the top of the flower. In both cases, the wire can be removed easily with a pair of pliers.

slowly and carefully pull it straight out through the top of the flower.

Phaleonopsis orchids are fastened with a loop of wire passed through the opening between the petals of the flower. After these wires are cut short, the wire is very easy to remove.

The short, thick stems of cattleya and cymbidium orchids are sometimes inserted into vials of water, or else the flowers have a piece of wire inserted straight up into the thick stem. Although the wires are tightly wedged, they are easy to remove.

If flowers from the groom's boutonniere are to be pressed, they must be separated from the bouquet and carefully labelled for identification so that they do not become confused with the flowers in the bride's bouquet.

Wedding bouquets are usually mounted on holders with curved handles. A facial tissue box with an opening in the center makes an excellent stand for the bouquet. If you keep the bouquet standing upright in the tissue box, the flowers will not become bruised while lying against the workbench.

Cut four or five flowers from the bouquet and prepare them for the press as required for that particular flower. Detailed instructions for pressing flowers can be found in the Alphabetical Guide. Do not remove all the flowers at one time. They will hold up better if they keep company with each other while waiting to be pressed.

Leaves, fern, and baby's breath, which are hardier than flowers, can be pressed last. If the night is wearing on and you are wearing out, foliage and baby's breath, as well as some hardy flowers, can be left overnight in a plastic bag in the refrigerator and completed the next day. Cymbidium orchids can almost always be held over with safety. White roses, however, should never be held over.

Work Area

You will need an area to work with that has space for the design, your supplies, and your tools. The workbench and chair should be at a comfortable height, so as not to put a strain on your back. An exhaust fan or air purifier should be available in the room to remove the particles of powdered chalk from the air. Avoid prolonged inhalation of chalk particles.

Your remuneration for pressed preserved wedding bouquets can be adequate or rather profitable, depending upon the degree of skill and speed that you have developed. For one who has acquired the necessary skills, an average bouquet should require about three to four hours for preparing the flowers for the presses, and around four to five hours for reassembling, arranging, mounting, and framing the bouquet.

Carnations and roses, the most popular flowers used in wedding bouquets, are also the most tedious because their petals must be dismantled and reassembled if color is to be preserved. Though one might balk at the prospect of so te-

dious an effort, it will require no more patience than that which you might need in working delicate embroidery or needlepoint.

Reassembling the Flowers

Gather together all the vegetation from the presses—rose petals, carnation petals, baby's breath, ribbons, and doily. Reassemble the individual flowers as necessary. Apply paint to stephanotis or gardenias if these were in the bouquet.

After all the flowers have been reassembled, check the sketch and notes. Count the flowers to see that they are the correct number.

Prepare any accoutrements that were in the bouquet such as a doily, ribbons, bows, or net tufts (instructions follow).

When all the parts of the bouquet have been gathered together, the bouquet is ready to be arranged against the background fabric chosen by the bride and then mounted in a frame of her choosing.

Preparing Lace Doily

Lace doilies for a bride's bouquet are sewn onto the plastic holders. The doily must be cut from the holder about 1½″ from the outer edge and ironed flat.

Illus. 11-2. When a lace doily is included in a bouquet, it must be cut up and reassembled in order to work in a two-dimensional format. You will need only enough of the lace to give the impression of a doily behind the pressed-flower arrangement.

Cut the strip of lace into 2″- or 3″-wide pie-shaped wedges (Illus. 11–2). Discard the scraps from between the wedges.

Preparing Ribbons

For ribbon loops hanging below the flowers, cut ribbon about 15″ long. Bring two ends of the ribbon together to form a loop and then iron it flat. The loop will have square corners at the bottom (Illus 11–3a).

For ribbon streamers, cut ribbon about 8″ long. If the ribbon has a cut edge (without a selvage), a slight curve can be ironed into the ribbon (Illus. 11–3b) by stretching one side of the ribbon as the iron passes over it. If the ribbon has a tight selvage or it is double-faced satin edged with picot, it might be difficult to stretch the ribbon into a curve. In this case, a fold pressed into the ribbon (Illus. 11–3c) will give the appearance of a curl as it hangs down from the bouquet. Straight ribbons used alongside the looped and curved ribbons are effective for contrast.

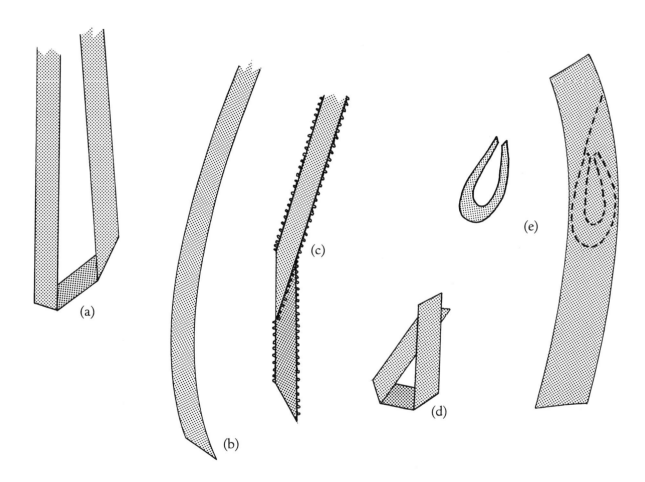

Illus. 11-3a through e. Ribbons can be prepared in several ways for preserved wedding bouquets. In examples a & b, ironed-in folds give the impression of loops. In example c, a curve has been ironed in to the ribbon by pulling on one side. Example d was ironed with a twist in it and example e was simply cut into the shape of a loop.

Remove the bows from the bouquet and iron them flat.

To simulate bows in a bouquet, you can iron narrow ribbon into loops or cut wide ribbon into rounded arches.

To make simulated bows, first cut several lengths of ribbon about 4″ long. Bring the two ends of each ribbon together to form a loop and iron it flat. Each loop will have square corners (Illus. 11–3d).

If the ribbon is fairly wide, it can be cut into arches. These arches (Illus. 11–3e) will be a fair representation of the loops of ribbon in a bouquet.

Preparing Nylon Net Tufts

In a bride's bouquet, net tufts are made from rectangles of net about 4″ × 8″ that are gathered together with a twist of wire. The net must be reworked to simulate the effect of fluffy tufts of net in this new flat medium. Remove the wire and iron the rectangles of net flat. Fold the rectangular pieces of net in half lengthwise (Illus. 11–4a).

CUTTING THE NET

Cut through these pieces of net to make two or three triangular pieces from each folded rectangle, keeping the folded edges of the triangles intact (Illus. 11–4b). Discard the scraps between triangles.

Cut into the open ends of each triangle to make three points or teeth (Illus. 11–4c). Do not cut all the way down through the folded edge of the net. Discard scraps between the points.

Hold the folded side of the toothed triangles between your thumb and forefinger and twist slightly to separate the uneven edges. When you are finished, six points will be visible, giving the pieces of net a tufted appearance.

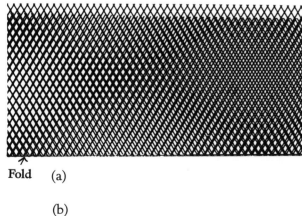

Fold   (a)

(b)

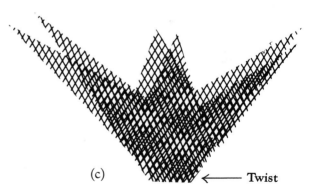

(c)   ←——— **Twist**

Illus. 11-4a through c. To make net tufts, fold the netting in half (a), draw several three-toothed wedges (b), cut them out, and twist (c) to create puffs of netting.

PRESSING THE NET TUFTS

After reworking all the net tufts in this manner, place them in a thin padded pressboard, cover them with plain chipboard, and put them in the basic press for a few hours. Net tufts can be un-ruly and difficult to work because the points have a tendency to curl. After the tufts have been in the press for a few hours, they will be easier to handle.

ARRANGING NET TUFTS

If netting was used around the outer edge of the bouquet as a doily, place the pressed net tufts on the background fabric before arranging the flowers. Lay the tufts down where the outer edges of the flowers will be, as a lacy doily would

be worked. If net was used among the flowers, insert the tufts between flowers and leaves after they are in place. Press down against the lower end of a flower or a leaf, thus raising the top edge just enough to slip the net tuft underneath.

Preparing a Lace Fan

Dismantle the fan by first carefully removing the lace from its hard plastic ribs. Discard the plastic skeleton. If a lace border trim was glued along the top and sides of the fan, remove this also. Iron both the lace and the border.

Lay the lace across one corner of the picture (Illus. 11–5), adjusting for extra fullness so that it fits comfortably into its allotted space—wide at

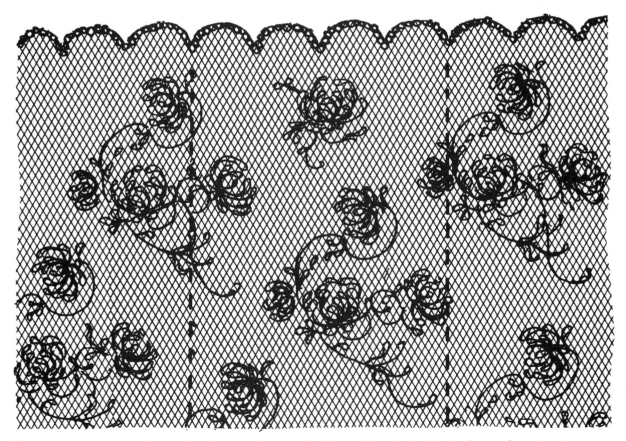

Illus. 11-5. You can simulate a lace fan in a bouquet by dismantling it, ironing it flat, and cutting it into three pieces, as shown. Discard the hard plastic ribs because they cannot be used in the pressed arrangement.

Illus. 11-6. Arrange the pieces of lace in the shape of a fan. Cut the bottom pieces into wedges to recreate the folds at the base of the fan. Make simulated ribs out of heavy paper cut in ¼-inch strips.

the top and very narrow at the base. Pin tucks into the lace as needed to maintain the proper shape. Secure the tucks with stitches and trim away the excess fabric formed by the tucks (Illus. 11–6).

Cut away excess length at the bottom of the fan.

REWORKING THE RIBS OF THE FAN

To simulate the ribs of the fan that have been discarded, cut heavy paper into strips about ¼″ wide and the length of the lace. Glue these strips on the back of the lace, evenly spaced, with each spoke meeting at the bottom center of the fan.

Glue or stitch the lace border to the fan.

Preparing a Simulated Bible or Prayer Book

You may have to recreate a bouquet that was carried on a Bible or prayer book. These can be simulated with white file cards and 1″-wide gold ribbon (Illus. 11–7). It is best to mount this style bouquet in a 12″ × 24″ rectangular frame, because the curved edge of an oval frame would clash with the straight edge of the book.

Cut two unlined white file cards so that they measure 7″ × 3″. Then cut one end at an angle so that one side measures 6½″ long. These will represent the cover of the book.

Cut a 1″ gold paper ribbon to a 6¾″ length. This will represent the gold-edged pages of the book. For perspective, cut a slight inward curve at both ends of the ribbon.

Glue ribbon along the longest edge of one of the cards, allowing a small margin of the card to protrude beyond the ribbon.

Glue the second piece of card on top of these, allowing the gold "pages" to show between the two white covers.

Do not mount thick parts of flowers, such as the stumps of roses, on top of the file cards, because they will not be properly supported. Thin rose petals can safely be displayed against the file cards.

Some of the 3″ width of the file card can be trimmed away as necessary, provided that pressed materials cover up the area of the cut.

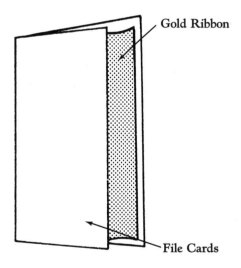

Illus. 11-7. Make a simulated bible or prayer book with two file cards and some gold paper.

Gold Ribbon

File Cards

Preparing Novelties Used in Bouquets

Pearl baby's breath   Cut the wire stems off the clusters of pearls and arrange them around the outside edges of the bouquet, away from the flowers.

Pearl hearts   Cut wire stems off the hearts and arrange them in the lower part of the bouquet positioned next to the groom's boutonniere.

Pearl corsage pins used in stephanotis These should always be omitted.

Butterflies   These are usually mounted on a heavy lump of wire and net. First cut off the wire stem and then tap gently on the lump with a hammer to flatten it out a little. Arrange the butterflies around the outer edges of the bouquet, away from the flowers.

Plastic flowers   These are too thick and rigid to be used among the pressed flowers and should always be omitted.

Plastic leaves   The circle of leaves used under gardenias are very flat and can be used in the picture under the flowers, if you wish. Simply trim away the lower part of the leaves so that only the points are visible.

Silk flowers   These are generally manufactured with plastic stems, calyxes, and stamens, making them almost as unusable as plastic flowers. If the plastic parts of the flowers can be removed, the silk petals can be used very well among the pressed flowers.

Leafless bouquets   Occasionally a bouquet is made up all flowers, having no leaves or fern whatsoever. Net tufts or ribbons are sometimes used between the flowers. If the ribbons and netting are not sufficient to cover the stumps of the dried flowers, use pressed rose leaves as sparingly as possible to cover them.

Special Effects

Florists dream up all kinds of clever and unusual designs, always striving to create a better, more beautiful, and more unusual effect for their bridal bouquets. Just when I think I've seen everything, a bouquet with a clever new innovative use of flowers shows up at my front door to keep me on my toes.

For one such trick, a small rose is embedded into the hollow center of a carnation. To reproduce this effect, reassemble the rose petals without the calyx, using tape at the base of the petals to hold them together. Cut a slit in the center of a circle of carnation petals that have been affixed to masking tape.

Insert the rose through the slit. Place loose carnation petals all around the rose. When pink roses are used inside a carnation, all is well, but when a yellow pressed rose is inserted into a pressed white carnation, it looks a bit like a fried egg. For this color scheme, use an oval arrangement of carnation petals with the rose protruding up beyond the top of the carnation.

Florists also create contrived flowers called *glamellias* from the petals of a gladiolus. Many layers of gladiolus petals are glued together to make a flower anywhere from 4″ to 8″ in diameter. When dismantling these flowers, the glue may tear the lower part of the petals, but this will not interfere with their final presentation.

Florists sometimes spray colored paint on flowers also. This can present a problem. On roses, the paint is only on the outer petals. These must often be discarded if they have withered. Mix chalk to match the color of the paint and dust the remaining petals with the colored chalk.

Carnations or chrysanthemums that have been sprayed with paint are a little more manageable. All or most of the petals will have paint on them, providing permanent color for the pressed bouquet. Dust the petals with chalk mixed to match the paint as an aid to drying and to color the unpainted lower halves of the petals.

During heat waves, roses can open full blown before the ceremony begins and begin to droop unattractively. To prevent this, florists use a sticky spray that prevents the flowers from opening. This renders useless the outer petals, but if luck is on your side, the petals in the center of the flowers will still be usable.

Though it is tempting to issue directives to florists, saying "don't do this," and "don't do that," remember that theirs is a highly competitive business, and they must use every trick in the trade to keep ahead.

Nor can you request the florists to refrain from using wax in the center of gardenias. This is done by the grower not the florist.

I do object to a glue that florists use to paste flowers on top of leaves or to glue leaves to the sides of flowers. In most cases, the glue can be coaxed off the petals, but this can be time consuming. Several times, I have been unable to remove the glue and the flowers had to be discarded. Or else the petals tore and had to be hidden from view.

Four Bouquet Examples

THE NOSEGAY (Illus. 11–8 through 11–12)

When flowers, leaves, and baby's breath are evenly distributed, no sketch to indicate placement of the flowers is necessary. Besides the bouquet's floral composition, the sketch in Illus. 12–8 shows the doily, ribbon streamers, and bows in the center of the bouquet, a note to include the invitation, and the size of the bouquet. The groom's boutonniere is noted below the sketch.

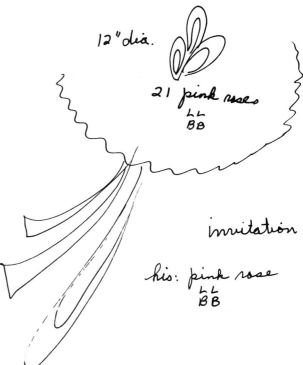

Illus. 11-8. Each time you receive a bouquet to preserve, make a sketch of its composition. This will be an invaluable aid when you reassemble the many parts.

Illus. 11–9 and 11–10. The approximate location of the completed bouquet is first roughed out with wedges of lace from the doily. Each wedge overlaps the next so as to give the lace a ruffled effect when viewed in perspective. Ribbon streamers and loops are then placed below and under the lace doily so that they appear to be coming out from under the bouquet. The wedding invitation is placed on the background fabric before the flowers are arranged so that it will be in close proximity to the bouquet. Roses pressed with sepals down are used in the center of the bouquet and profile roses pressed with sepals up are used around the outer edge. The sepals of the profile roses, radiating outward, contribute to direction and movement in an arrangement. Fern is then added to the groom's boutonniere and inserted around the perimeter of the bouquet.

Illus. 11–11 and 11–12. Baby's breath, that has been pressed in clusters, is pushed in little bunches around the outer edges of the bouquet and in between the flowers and leaves to complete the bouquet.

This wedding invitation was encircled with an arrangement of pressed pear blossoms, doubled for fullness and colored with felt-pen ink, and jasmine leaves.

Specialty items, designed by a manufacturer, that can be used to display pressed-flower arrangements. Included here are a vanity set and a locket.

A pretty picture, isn't it? But not for long! One year after its completion, most of the flowers in this design will have lost all of their color.

This lily and this daffodil were dismantled, pressed in individual pieces, and then reassembled to give them an interesting illusion of depth (right). A botanical study of the zinnia (bottom right) shows the growth pattern of the various parts of this flower. This ten-year-old design (bottom left) includes vanda orchids and flowers that were contrived from the petals of the gladiolus.

L

(Left) Pressed materials in this ten-year-old design include wild radish, rose geranium, Queen Anne's lace, maidenhair fern, and grass gone to seed. The vase was fashioned from curved blades of festuca grass.

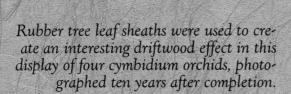

Rubber tree leaf sheaths were used to create an interesting driftwood effect in this display of four cymbidium orchids, photographed ten years after completion.

M

Pressed-flower decorations for stationery are limited only by the imagination. The examples shown here have been further enhanced with the addition of lines drawn with felt pens.

For simple, elegant correspondence, floral stationery is easy to make using pressed flowers glued directly onto the paper (top).

The greeting cards, bookmarks, address book, and wooden box have all been made more attractive with the addition of pressed-flower designs sealed under plastic laminating film and shellac (left).

The round growth pattern of Queen Anne's lace was recreated by using both full-face and profile florets, the latter of which appear to retreat from view (left). The pearblossoms and cotoneaster leaves in this arrangement (bottom left) still retain their color eleven years after completion. Both chalk and felt-pen ink were used to fix the color on the petals of this bird of paradise, photographed nine years after completion (bottom right).

THE CASCADE (Illus. 11–13 through 11–17)

Details in the tail of this cascade have been sketched to carefully note the locations of the individual flowers. It was particularly important to duplicate the arrangement of the flowers in the tail. Carnations were placed throughout the tail, but roses were located only in the upper portion. In the body of the bouquet, the flowers and leaves were evenly distributed, so details were not necessary. The doily is shown, however. The groom's boutonniere was noted to the right of the sketch.

Illus. 11–14. *The approximate dimensions of the completed cascade are bounded by wedges of lace from the doily. An opening is left between them for the flowers that will cascade below the body of the bouquet. Ribbon streamers and loops are arranged so that their edges will be under the flowers.*

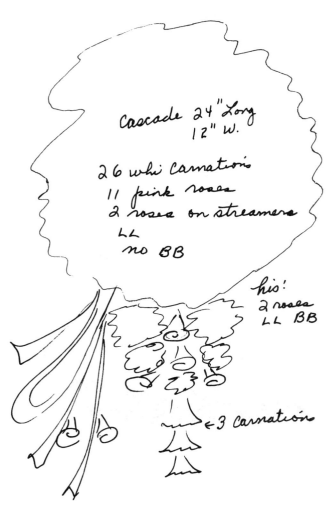

Illus. 11-13. *This sketch of a cascade bouquet includes such information as its dimensions, the makeup of the cascade portion, the placement of ribbons, and the types of flowers in the groom's boutonniere.*

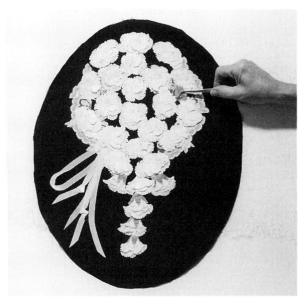

Illus. 11–15. *Round carnations are used in the middle of the body and oval-shaped carnations in the outer parts of the bouquet for perspective. Profile carnations, used in the tail of the bouquet, contribute to line and direction. Pink sweetheart roses are tucked in between the carnations so that their raw stumps will be hidden.*

Illus. 11–16. Roses have been placed throughout the bouquet, and leaves are now being added. Roses at the top of the bouquet face up, and roses at the bottom face down, giving the arrangement line and direction.

FLOWERS CARRIED ON A BIBLE
(Illus. 11–18 through 11–23)

This sketch shows two parallel lines to indicate a Bible. The placement of the orchids is shown simply as titled circles, because these flowers are too time consuming to sketch. Leaves around the orchids are noted and the locations of the roses are sketched briefly. The note "no BB" has been made because a bouquet that has no baby's breath is uncommon.

The distribution of stephanotis has also been noted—five over the book and fourteen in the tail. The 10″ length of tail has been noted along with a few lines to indicate the location of ribbons. Though the notes indicate no leaves in the tail, I included snippets of leaves for continuity. The groom's boutonniere is noted in the lower left hand corner.

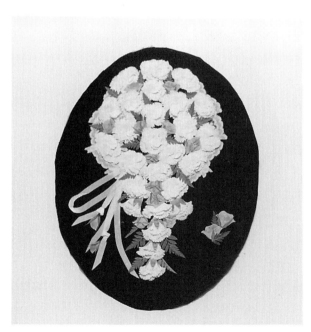

Illus. 11–17. The bouquet is completed by inserting fern between the flowers. The base of each leaf faces towards the center, and each point projects outward. The groom's boutonniere has been arranged in the lower right-hand corner.

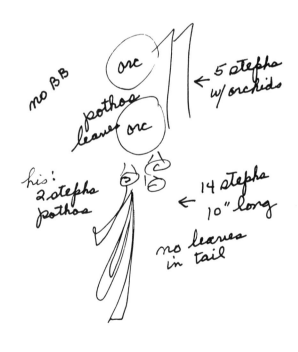

Illus. 11-18. A sketch of a bouquet that was mounted on a bible. The pressed-flower version of the bouquet will include a simulated prayer book made from file cards and gold ribbon.

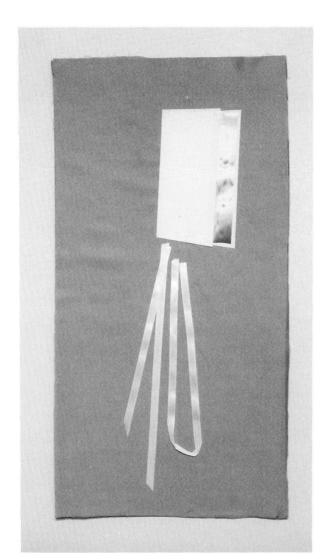

Illus. 11–20. A general rule to follow when constructing a bouquet is to first place the largest or most important flowers in the bouquet—in this case, two cattleya orchids.

Illus. 11–19. The simulated Bible, made from white file cards and gold ribbon, is placed on the background fabric, and ribbons and streamers are arranged in the approximate position of the bouquet. Adjustments can be made to these features as the bouquet takes shape.

Illus. 11–22. Some of the stephanotis have been joined to their interesting calyxes. These are especially effective in a cascading bouquet such as this. Some of the stephanotis have been pressed in full face, some in profile, and others have been trimmed to give an interesting three-quarter view. The white roses have begun to be added.

Illus. 11–21. Pothos leaves have been added, some trimmed with the curve cutting tool for a variety of shapes. Positioning of stephanotis has begun. The stumps of these flowers were hidden under the ribbons and leaves, as necessary.

FLOWERS CARRIED ON A FAN
(Illus. 11–24 through 11–29)

In Illus. 16–24, cymbidium orchids, roses, and ribbon streamers are sketched to show location, and the presence of baby's breath and ivy leaves are noted. Although baby's breath was used throughout the original bouquet, I took the liberty of using it only around the outside because it detracted from the visibility of the orchids in the interior of the pressed arrangement. The groom's boutonniere is indicated at lower left of sketch.

Illus. 11–23. The groom's boutonniere is placed in the lower right-hand corner. The pothos leaves have been trimmed with the curved cutting tool for a better appearance. The three roses were added last, with the stumps of these flowers hidden under vegetation and ribbons.

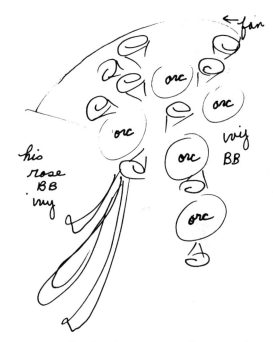

Illus. 11-24. This sketch maps out a bouquet that was mounted on a fan, which will be replaced by a two dimensional version for the preserved bouquet.

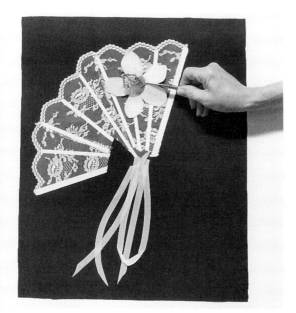

Illus. 11–25. The lace from the fan, reworked and fitted with simulated paper ribs, is placed on the background fabric along the lines of the original bouquet, as are the streamers and ribbons. One cymbidium orchid is positioned according to the sketch.

Illus. 11–27. Ivy leaves are inserted around the outer edges of the bouquet and between the flowers, employing them as needed to cover the stumps of the roses. Smaller leaves are arranged as they might appear at the end of a spray.

Illus. 11–26. After all the orchids were in place, roses were added with those at the top of the fan facing upwards and those at the bottom facing downwards. These placements give line and direction to the piece.

Illus. 11–28. Baby's breath is always inserted last when reconstructing a bouquet.

Illus. 11–29. The completed bouquet.

Durability of Wedding Bouquets

DRAMATICALLY PERISHABLE FLOWERS

Some flowers used in wedding bouquets, such as alstroemeria, sweet william, and sweet pea, will lose all their color one year after they have been pressed and exposed to light. Lilacs will turn rust red after one year. Chalk does not forestall aging in these flowers. Tulips and freesias are questionable, although I have not observed these flowers for any length of time.

CARNATIONS

Unlike roses, if red carnations are dusted with bright red chalk, they dry a true red, and retain their color for many years. Be aware, however, that red chalk is messy. You must be fastidious as you work or you will find red stains all over yourself, the workbench, and the floor. Even though this flower can be dried a true red, as compared to the burgundy color of dried red roses, the rose is much preferred over the carnation by most brides.

White and pale-colored carnations, even when treated with chalk, will not hold their color well. Aging will begin to be evident in about four years. Darker colors hold up much better when treated with chalk to match the color of the live flower, aging to lighter versions of their original colors.

When florists use commercially dyed carnations in a wedding bouquet, the dye results in permanent color in the pressed flower. Chalk or cornstarch should be applied to these flowers as an aid to drying. Parts of the flower that have not been colored with dye or chalk will age to beige in four years.

CHRYSANTHEMUMS

The petals of large white mum daisies, when treated with chalk, gradually turn to toast color after four or five years. Colored mum daisies that have been treated with chalk to match the color of the flower hold up much better.

White and colored china mums hold up well, but they are seldom used in wedding bouquets because they have a tendency to shatter when wired.

Small, white spider mums, or wedding mums, seem to hold up fairly well, but I have not observed them beyond three years.

GARDENIAS

It is possible to dry these flowers with a nice, creamy white color if chalk is applied to the live flowers, and they are dried in a microwave oven. However, the natural color of these flowers is dramatically perishable. Chalk does not stabilize the color and the flowers quickly age with uneven gray blotches within the second year.

GLADIOLUS

White gladiolus, treated with white chalk, show signs of age in four years, while colored gladiolus hold up longer with the addition of chalk. Discoloration in these flowers can be quite attractive because the petals begin to darken in the center, adding a marvelous appearance of depth to the flower.

LEAVES

Maranta, or prayer plant, leaves, with their bright green coloring and red tracery, are sometimes used in a bouquet for a dramatic effect. This leaf can be dried in a microwave oven, which will successfully preserve its color. However, the color and its dramatic effect will be gone after one year's exposure to light. Because foliage always discolors after one year, this will be true of any leaves that are featured prominently in a bouquet's design.

ORCHIDS

When treated with chalk, orchids will retain their color for many years.

ROSES

I have never succeeded in preserving the bright color of red roses, but I believe it might be possible with the help of a chemist. In one of my earlier experiments a bright red spot remained on an otherwise darkened red rose petal, but I was never able to repeat the accident. Red chalk does not stabilize the color of these flowers. They always dry a burgundy, or maroon red, sometimes even darker. The burgundy color holds up well over the years. I have observed good color still present after ten years in commercially grown red roses that have been pressed.

This kind of durability is not true of the single-variety wild rose found growing along the roadside. These red roses turn rust red in the second year. As with other categories of flowers, the durability of color in a particular species of rose has no relationship to durability of color in others just because they are all in the rose family.

As a background color, the burgundy or maroon color of pressed red roses looks well against off-white. If the bouquet is made up of red and white roses, the choice of background becomes more difficult. I have found that a dusty pink background both complements the burgundy colored roses and affords enough contrast to show white roses, as well.

Peachy-pink sonia roses are very popular with brides and florists alike. Their chalked color holds up well in preserved wedding bouquets. When dried without chalk, they dry a more red color.

Some wedding bouquets include the sterling silver rose. I have not personally observed the aging process of this flower, but a bride reports that the color of her sterling silver roses is holding up well after five years.

Talisman roses, seldom used in wedding bouquets, have durable color when treated with chalk. This flower has a dual-colored petal and gives a very effective appearance in its pressed form because the cuffs turn down on each petal and contrast with the rest of the flower, adding depth and perspective.

On hot days, fresh white roses are extremely perishable in wedding bouquets. The petals wilt and turn brown. Brides should keep the bouquet in an air-conditioned room during the reception if possible, but *not* in the caterer's refrigerator. Refrigerators meant to store food are too cold and can result in frostbitten flowers. White roses, when subjected to heavy doses of cigarette smoke, develop black stains around the edges of their petals.

When white roses have been treated with white chalk, they hold up quite well over the years, whereas pale yellow and pale pink roses fade in a few years. Darker pinks and darker yellow roses, when treated with chalk, age to light pink and light yellow.

The small, light pink sweetheart rose, when pressed without chalk, darkens to a mulberry color. For wedding bouquets, the color can be stabilized with the addition of chalk.

STEPHANOTIS

These flowers can be dried with a nice creamy white color when treated with chalk and dried in the microwave. However, the natural color of these flowers is dramatically perishable. Chalk does not stabilize the color and they quickly age to a toast color.

Alphabetic Guide

The pressing technique that I have found most successful follows the name of each flower in this guide. Each flower is graded for durability of color—Best, Excellent, Good, Fair, or Poor. If durability is omitted, it is because I have not had an opportunity to observe the flower's aging process. The list is, of necessity, limited to flowers that can be grown in southern California, where I live. Others, that might be very good subjects for pressing, are not listed because they are not available to me.

If a flower that you want to press is not listed, try pressing it with the new methods you have learned. Start with the basic press. If discoloration occurs, add heat. If discoloration persists, add chalk, less weight, or microwaves, until one or a combination of these gives good results. It may take a little experimentation, depending on how stubborn the flower might be. After you have found a successful formula for pressing the flower, be sure to test the flower on a sunny windowsill to determine the durability of its color, and also keep records for future reference.

BEST NATURAL COLOR

This category includes flowers whose natural color is exceptionally durable. In some of these flowers and leaves, fading may not occur for six to eight years.

Flowers dyed with felt-pen ink can be considered as durable as those in Best Natural Color category, so long as the flowers are not displayed in a window where the direct rays of the sun will bleach away all the color.

For quick reference, I have included here a summary of flowers with exceptionally durable natural color.

Blue:
Bachelor Button—dark blue (sometimes unreliable)
Delphinium—dark blue
Forget-me-not
Johnny-jump-up
Larkspur—dark blue
Lobelia—dark blue

Lavender:
Ivy Leaf Geranium
Pelargonium Peltatum
Rose Geranium

Pink:
English Daisy

Purple:
Geranium Madam Layal (Pansy Geranium). The two dark purple petals of this flower can be rated Best, but color in the pale lavender petals is not durable.
Statice
Wild Radish

Bright Red:
Geranium Flower Spring—a variegated green/white leafed plant that bears salmon red single flowers. Florets are sparse with heads displaying only a few florets at a time.
Pomegranate

Dark Red:
Verbena
English Daisy

Mulberry Red:
Sweetheart rose—a small pink rose available

through florists. Dries a deep rose or mulberry color.

White:
 Alyssum
 Candytuft
 Larkspur
 Paludosum Daisy
 Statice

White/Gray:
 Acacia leaves
 Dusty Miller leaves
 Cotoneaster leaves (reverse white flannel side)

Yellow:
 Coreopsis
 Marigold, dwarf French
 Multicaule Mum

EXCELLENT

Flowers in this category have admirable natural color durability, though not quite on a par with those in the Best category.

Also in this category are flowers whose natural coloring is poor, because they can be upgraded to Excellent if dusted with chalk before pressing. Orchids and white roses fall into this category.

GOOD

In this category are flowers with poor natural coloring that can be upgraded to Good when dusted with chalk before pressing. Carnations are in this category.

FAIR

In this category are flowers whose natural color fades a little after one year but which retain a

small amount of color for one or two years thereafter. Pansies are in this category. These cannot ordinarily be dusted with chalk to upgrade them to Good or Excellent.

POOR

This category includes flowers whose natural color either bleaches away entirely or turns to rust red after one year. It also includes flowers that become transparent after they have dried.

However, with the exception of flowers that turn rust red, flowers in this category can be considered as durable as those in Best Natural Color when dyed with felt-pen ink. Felt-pen ink will not hide discoloration in flowers that age to rust red.

The following is an easy reference list of flowers and leaves that cannot be dried successfully without using the microwave oven.

Flowers:
 Cymbidium orchid
 Dendrobium orchid
 Gardenia
 Lily-of-the-valley
 Mum daisy
 Rubrum lily
 Stephanotis

Leaves:
 Algerian ivy
 Asparagus fern
 Chinese evergreen (aglaonema modestum)
 Dieffenbachia
 Pothos
 Prayer plant (maranta leuconeura)

Key to Symbols:

 Press flowers in basic press

 Press flowers in borax mattress press

 Dust flowers with chalk

 Dry flowers in oven

 Color flowers with felt-pen ink

 Dry flowers in microwave

 Press flowers in a book

List of Flowers

Acacia Flower   Book. Flowers age to rust.

Acacia Leaf   Book. Fern-like gray leaves have very nice appearance and are one of the best for color durability. Heavy, woody stems can disfigure the delicate petals of flowers lying on top of these leaves. Use with caution. See Undergrowth in Chapter 9.

African Orchid Tree Flower (Bauhinia)   Basic press with heat. Color durability is Excellent. Ages to pretty peach with lovely tracery of venation.

Ageratum   Basic press. Color durability is Fair.

Air Fern   Book. Color durability is Good. Retains green coloring for about three years.

Algerian Ivy   Microwave to prevent white markings from turning brown. Microwave three leaves in one padded pressboard for two minutes on ¾ power. If white is the dominant color, white

chalk may need to be dusted on the leaves before subjecting them to microwaves. Finish drying in basic press with heat. May blister if microwave power is too high. Used in wedding bouquets occasionally. Color durability is Poor.

Alstroemeria   Microwave and basic press with heat. Pinch off excess buds and flowers so that they are not overlapping. Microwave one spray in one sandwich on ¾ power for two minutes. Let stand 10 minutes under pressure. Repeat microwave until petals are dry. Finish drying stem and calyx in basic press with heat. Occasionally used in wedding bouquets. Color durability is Poor.

Alyssum   Basic press. Color durability is Best for white and Poor for lavender.

Anemone   Basic press in oven. Dust with chalk.

Anthurium   Microwave. Remove pistil from flower petal. Dust petal with bright red chalk. Microwave one petal in one padded pressboard for two minutes on ¾ power. Split pistil in half to reduce bulk. Press in basic press. Reconstruct flower. Color durability is Poor.

Arborvitae   Book. Color durability is Poor.

Asparagus Fern   Microwave several sprays in each of three thin padded pressboards on ¾ power for two minutes. A stack of three sand-wiches can be dried in the microwave at one time. Asparagus fern is one of the few plants that can be dried successfully in a microwave with this much added bulk. Finish drying in basic press with heat. Color durability is Poor.

Azalea   Basic press. Color durability is Poor.

Baby's Breath   Book. For wedding bouquets, cut small sprays of flowers with stems no longer than 2″ and gather them together between your thumb and forefinger. Pinch the flowers flat and press tiny nosegays between the pages of a book with a brick for pressure.

When baby's breath from a wedding bouquet has arrived dry and brittle, it can be revived in the refrigerator. Put the flowers in a plastic bag with a dab of water and seal the bag tightly. If too much moisture is present in the bag, the flowers could develop mould. Leave the flowers in the refrigerator for a day. Color durability is Best, but does not dry a sharp white.

Bachelor's Button (Centaurea Cyanus) Basic Press. Press in thick pressboard with heat.

This flower can be dismantled to press individ-ual lily-shaped florets in a book. Very nice to use where tiny flowers are needed.

It is claimed that these dark blue flowers, used in King Tut's funerary wreath, still showed evi-

dence of their blue coloring when his tomb was opened thousands of years after his burial. Color durability is Best for dark blue, although this is sometimes unreliable. Poor for pink.

Bird of Paradise (Strelitzia)   Book and basic press with heat.
Preparing the Flower

(Illus. AG–1). Remove orange and blue petals and dust orange petals with chalk. Press both orange and blue petals in book with brick for weight.

Cut pods off stem about 1½″ below curve. Split pod in two and scrape out pithy material at the base of the pod and any extra growth inside the pod. Dip beak of pod in boiling water to make it more pliable so it can be spread flat on padded pressboard. Press in basic press with heat.

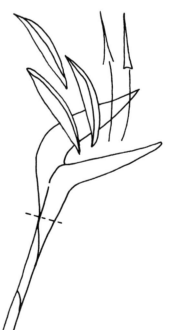

Illus. AG-1. To prepare a Bird of Paradise for press-ing, remove the orange and blue petals and cut the pod from the stem.

Stems of this flower are overlapping layers of leaf-like sheaths. Remove sheaths and dip in boiling water so they can be more easily flattened. Press in basic press or book with heat.

Reassembling Flower

Color orange and blue petals with felt-pen ink. Cut a slit close to the top edge of the beak-like pod. Insert petals into slit. Arrange sheaths of stem below pod. Durability of natural color is Poor.

Borage   Basic press. Color durability is Poor.

Boston Fern   Basic press. Color durability is Poor.

Bougainvillea   Book. Color durability is Poor.

Calendula   Basic press. Color durability is Fair.

Campanula   Basic press. Color durability is Poor.

Canarybird Bush (Crotalaria Agatiflora) Very good subject for pressing. Grows in mild climates and tolerates mild frost. Looks like hummingbird when stem left intact, for a whimsical touch.

Candytuft (Iberis)   Basic press. Flower head splays open unattractively when pressed whole.

The little two-petalled florets are very nice touches where tiny flowers are needed. Care must be used when arranging a series of these florets around the outer edges of an arrangement. They have a tendency to look like a swarm of gnats. Dries sharp white. Color durability is one of the Best.

Cape Honeysuckle Flower   Basic press. Color durability is Poor.

Cape Honeysuckle Leaf   Book. Very nice shape, similar to rose leaves. This is a good leaf to use commercially when production is up and you need a large number of leaves. Color durability is Poor.

Carnation   Pressboard with brick weight. This flower is impossible to press whole without damaging shape and color. The petals fuse together into a blob and become indistinguishable from one another. Also, carnations retain a great deal of systemic moisture, and the multiple layers of moist petals lying against each other in a press results in severe discoloration. Neither microwaves nor chemicals have been of any help in altering the nature of this flower. Carnations also shrink easily if sufficient pressure is not applied. To press carnations with any kind of success, the flower must be dismantled, dried, and reassembled.

Preparing the Flower for Full-Face View

Remove petals from the calyx and discard calyx. Cut away long shanks attached to bottom of petals (Illus. AG–2a).

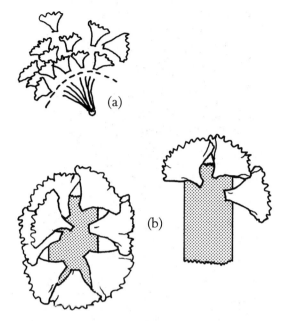

Illus. AG-2a & b. To prepare the carnation for full-face viewing, remove the petals from the calyx and cut away the long shanks (a). Then attach the petals to a piece of tape in a circular pattern (b).

Cut a piece of masking tape about ¾″ × 1½″ long. Holding the tape with sticky side up, attach petals all around the edges of the tape in a circular pattern (Illus. AG-2b).

Attach one more petal on the tape, slightly inside the first circle. Set taped petals aside.

Select 15 to 25 petals from those remaining and discard the rest.

Applying Chalk to the Petals

Drop all the loose petals and the sets of taped petals that were set aside earlier into a covered bowl of powdered tempera chalk mixed to match the color of the flower. Shake the bowl to distribute chalk on the petals.

Open the bowl and remove the loose and taped petals onto a piece of facial tissue, using a long tweezers to pick petals out of bowl. Shake off excess chalk as you remove them from the bowl. Rub chalk into the petals of the taped sets. Loose petals can survive without rubbing chalk into each petal, but if time permits, better results can be had if the chalk is rubbed into the petals as well.

Pressing the Petals

Lay the sets of taped petals face up on a padded pressboard and cover with a plain chipboard sheet. Sprinkle loose petals on a second padded pressboard and cover with a plain chipboard sheet.

Put a stack of three sandwiches in a gas oven with only the pilot for heat. Place a brick (do not use the basic press) on top of the stack of sandwiches for weight. The brick will absorb heat and transfer this heat to the petals to accelerate the drying process.

These flowers *must* be subjected to the direct heat from a warm brick so that they dry swiftly. If they do not dry within two days they can discolor. High heat, on the other hand, will scorch the petals.

Reassembling Carnations Full Face

Brush excess chalk from both the taped and loose petals. Insert and firmly seat one of the loose petals under the single petal that was taped below the outer circle of petals. Add a second and third petal by hooking their short stubby shanks, firmly seated, under the petal added previously (Illus. AG-3a).

Continue hooking each petal under its neighboring petal, moving around in an ever smaller center of the flower, until the opening can be covered with one last petal (Illus. AG-3b).

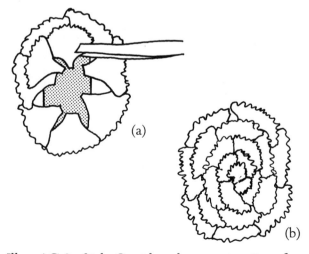

Illus. AG-3a & b. Complete the reconstruction of the flower by tucking subsequent petals underneath the ones added earlier (a). Finally, cover the opening in the center with a final petal.

To handle the reassembled flower, slip the prong of a tweezers under the middle of the flower, firmly grasping the center of the flower between the prongs. Do not tug on individual petals to move the flower.

For ease in handling, return taped, reconstructed flowers to basic press under pressure for 24 hours before using them in an arrangement.

Preparing the Flower for Profile View

Remove petals from calyx. If stem is attached, cut away the back of the stem to reduce bulk (Illus. AG–4a). Set calyx aside.

Cut away long shanks attached to bottom of the carnation petals (Illus. AG–4b).

Cut a piece of masking tape about ¾" wide × 1½" long. Holding the tape with sticky side up, attach three or four petals across the top of the narrow end of the tape, in a fan-like formation (Illus. AG–5).

Attach two more rows of petals to the tape, each row slightly lower than the preceding row.

Illus. AG-5. Attach the petals in rows halfway down the length of a 1½-inch piece of tape.

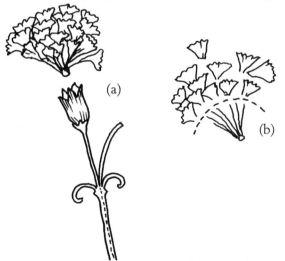

Illus. AG-4. To prepare a carnation for profile viewing, remove the petals from the calyx but do not throw the calyx and stem away. Cut away the shanks (b).

Fold lower end of the tape up and seal against the bottom edge of the last row of petals. Set taped petals aside.

Pressing the Calyx

Arrange calyxes, with or without stems attached, in a thin padded pressboard. Press in the basic press without heat. Heat dries the calyx

before it has a chance to flatten and will cause puckers and wrinkles. If a curve is desirable in the stem, you may need to tape it in place because the stems of carnations are quite stiff and rigid.

Reassembling Carnations in Profile

Brush excess chalk from taped petals and trim lower portion of masking tape to a point at their bases. Trim outer petals in a curve on both sides.

Insert taped petals into the calyx (Illus. AG–6), trimming to fit down inside the calyx to hide the tape. If necessary, insert a few extra petals to enhance fullness.

For ease in handling, return taped reconstructed flowers to basic press under pressure for 24 hours before using the flowers in an arrangement.

Reassembling Carnations Three-Quarter View

For ¾ view, attach the petals to the tape in an oval configuration instead of round circle. To create perspective in wedding bouquets, round carnations should be used in the center, oval carnations around the perimeter, and profiles in the lower portion of a cascade.

Illus. AG-6. After you have pressed the calyx and stem, slide in the set of taped petals.

Eleganté Carnations

The petals of these carnations are much smaller than the standard carnations and the flowers are only 1″ to 1½″ in diameter. When dismantling and reassembling eleganté carnations from a wedding bouquet, reassemble in their correct size.

Painted Carnations

Florists sometimes use spray paint on carnations. Powdered tempera chalk should be applied to match the paint as an aid to drying.

Dyed Carnations

Some carnations are dyed with a coloring agent that is absorbed through the stem of the flower and up into the veins, resulting in a multicolored flower, such as white with purple venation. The petals of these flowers can be treated with cornstarch as an aid to drying. The cornstarch can then be removed after the petals have dried.

Dual-Colored Carnations

Some carnations display a natural color that is either striped or edged with a second color. The edged flowers can be dipped in chalk to match the edge before the flower is dismantled.

Holding the petals of the flower tightly closed to prevent the colored chalk from staining the lower parts, dip the top of the petals in the chalk. Shake excess chalk from the petals. Proceed as directed for flowers of one color.

Drop the taped and loose petals into a bowl of chalk mixed to match the color of the lower portion of the flower (usually white).

Striped carnations can be dusted with cornstarch as an aid to drying.

Color Durability

White and light-colored carnations treated with chalk will begin to show discoloration after four years. Darker colored carnations that have been treated with chalk to match the flower will not discolor noticeably for a few more years.

Carnations colored with spray paint show discoloration only where paint is absent from the petals.

Carnations colored with dye absorbed through the stem of the flower show discoloration only between the veins in the petals.

Chinese Lantern Plant (Physalis) Basic press. Open flower and press flat for star-shaped flower. Color durability is Poor.

Chinese Evergreen Leaf (Aglaonema) Microwave one leaf in one padded pressboard for two minutes on ¾ power. Used in wedding bouquets occasionally. Color durability is Poor.

Chrysanthemum Microwave oven or borax mattress press. Chrysanthemums retain an exceptional amount of moisture and should not be pressed when freshly picked.

This family of flowers is extremely sensitive to bruising. Pressure applied too soon results in discoloration. Most flowers in the mum family can be dried in the borax mattress press. However, mum daisies require a microwave oven to dry without discoloration.

Preparing the Flower

Leave a small length of stem on the flower. Apply chalk to flower with a brush or shake in a covered bowl of powdered tempera chalk mixed to match the color of the flower.

If water has been sprinkled on the flowers and droplets of water are caught between the petals of these flowers, the chalk will be attracted to these droplets of water and dry into hard pebbles. Whenever a flower is being pressed, the flower should be as dry as possible at the outset. Water should be withheld from the flower before preparing it for the press.

Remove flower from chalk. Hold flower by the stem upside down over a wastebasket and shake out any excess chalk that might be lodged between the petals. Remove stem from flower.

Pressing Mums in Borax Mattress Press

With your thumb, make a depression in the borax mattress for each flower. Put the flowers face up on the borax mattress close together but not touching or overlapping. The thick calyx of each flower should be set in one of the depressions made in the borax mattress.

Cover the flowers with a blanket of fluffy polyester fibrefill. Put cover of the press on top but use no weight. Place press in an oven with only the pilot for heat.

Drying the Flowers

Flowers freshly cut require a longer time to dry. Flowers from wedding bouquets dry much faster.

Check flowers every day. When they are partially dry and beginning to feel crisp to the touch, remove the polyester fibrefill blanket. Carefully remove any strands of fibrefill that may have tangled in the petals of the flowers. Cover the flowers with double-knit fabric. Place polyester fibrefill blanket on top of the double-knit fabric. Put the cover on top of the press and add no more than five pounds of weight.

Check the flowers every day to see if they are dry all over. When all the petals are stiff and dry,

turn the flowers upside down on the borax mattress, avoiding the depressions made in the mattress pad. Cover the backs of the flowers with the polyester double-knit fabric, followed by a layer of polyester fibrefill. Replace cover on press and add weight of 20 pounds or so. Heat will no longer be necessary.

The petals of these flowers will not shrink, so the flowers can be flattened last as the last step, just a very slight bit of moisture remaining in the calyx. If there is more than a slight bit, the flower will discolor when weight is added. Any discoloration that occurs can be attributed to weights that have been added before the flowers were dry.

Removing Chalk from the Dried Flower

Brush excess chalk from the petals of the flowers. Lay the flower upside down on a piece of facial tissue and gently tap the back of the flower to shake loose any chalk caught between the petals. Blow loose chalk from the center of the flowers. If a substantial amount of chalk is left between the petals of these flowers, it will show up against the glass when the flowers are mounted in a picture. It is important to remove as much of the chalk as possible. Handle the flowers gently. They shatter when handled roughly.

Spider, Fuji, and Button Mums

When weight is applied to these flowers, the petals splay open to expose the calyx. Follow instructions given for other mums, but these flowers must be dried with absolutely no weight. When the flowers are completely and thoroughly dried (even the calyx), they can be turned upside down on the press and weights of 20 pounds or so can be added to flatten them.

Football Mums

The side petals of this flower hang down over the edge of the flower. These must be removed to thin down and flatten the shape of the flower. When petals around the outer edges of the flower are removed, the remainder of the petals are more loosely contained in the calyx and rough treatment could shake them loose. Chalk must be applied before removing petals, and the flower must be handled carefully. Use no weight on the press until the flowers have dried.

Daisy Mums

Prepare daisy mums in the same way as other mums.

Lay one piece of fluffy polyester fibrefill cut to same size on a thick padded pressboard. Place only *one* daisy mum face up on the thickly padded surface. Lay another piece of fluffy polyester fibrefill cut to fit pressboards against the face of the flower and cover with a plain sheet of chipboard (Illus. AG–7).

Place only *one* sandwich containing one daisy mum in microwave oven with marble weight. This mum, when dried in a microwave oven, tolerates pressure. Do not microwave more than one sandwich at a time. Microwave on ¾ power for one minute.

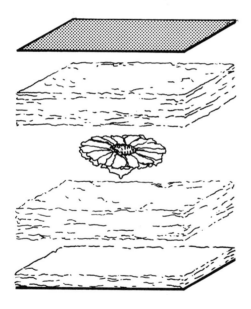

Illus. AG-7. Mum daisies must be dried in the microwave oven with a great deal of padding to prevent them from bruising. Only one flower can be pressed at a time.

Open sandwich immediately and remove polyester fibrefill from face of flower. If polyester fibrefill is not removed from the flower soon after it has been subjected to microwaves, the polyester fibres will fuse to the petals.

Put the plain piece of chipboard against the face of the flower. Let stand 30 minutes under pressure. If the petals of the flower are not dry—

microwave again with the chipboard still against the face of the flower. The flower must continue to receive pressure for 24 hours afterward.

Before using the flower in a picture, rub additional chalk into the petals for better color.

Color durability is Excellent for all mums, except daisy mums, for which it is Good.

Multicaule Mum

Basic press. Color durability is Best.

Cineraria   Basic press. Color durability is Poor.

Clematis   Basic press. Color durability is Poor.

Clematis Leaves and Buds   Basic press. Excellent shapes for pictures. Color durability is Poor.

Columbine (Aquilegia)   Basic press. Color durability is Poor.

Coralbell (Heuchera)   Basic press. Color durability is Poor.

Coreopsis   Basic press. Color durability is Best.

Cosmos   Basic press. Color durability is Fair for dark colors, Poor for pinks, and Excellent for yellow sulphureus.

Cotoneaster Leaf Book. Reverse side of one variety is nice grey color with flannel texture. Color durability is Best.

Daffodil

Preparing the Flower

Cut tall "cup" away from the "saucer" of petals. Cut the cup open so that it can be pressed flat (Illus. AG–8). Dust petals with chalk and press in basic press or book with heat.

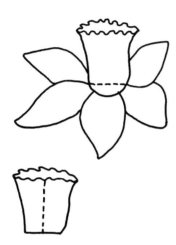

Illus. AG-8. To prepare a daffodil for pressing, cut away the cup and slice it open so that it can be pressed flat.

Reassembling Flower

For bright color and added durability, color petals with felt-pen ink.

Cut two U-shaped pieces from the length of petal that was the cup, as shown in Illus. AG–9.

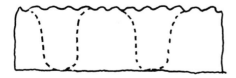

Illus. AG-9. Cut two U-shaped pieces from the cup and arrange them on the pressed petals.

Arrange the U-shaped petal on top of the set of saucer petals. Insert the second U-shaped petal behind the first so that it protrudes slightly above the front petal for perspective. Turn flower upside down on workbench and tape parts together with a small piece of masking tape. Durability of natural color is Poor.

Daisy Basic press. There are many varieties of flowers called daisies. Most can be pressed in the basic press. For large daisy mums, see Chrysanthemums. Color durability is Good.

Daisy, English (Bellis Perennis) Basic press. Color durability is Best for pink flowers.

Daisy, Marguerite Basic press. To coax a marguerite daisy to produce an oval center, allow the flower to become limp before pressing. Pinch the center together into an oval shape. Lay the flower face down against a plain sheet of chipboard and cover with a thick padded pressboard. Open the press in a few hours and check to see that the center of the flower is still an oval shape. If it has opened into its natural round shape, pinch again into an oval shape. The centers of these flowers are much too rigid and firm to form an oval shape without encouragement. Color durability is Fair.

Daisy, Paludosum Basic press. Color durability is Best.

Delphinium Basic press. Color durability: Best for dark blue flowers; Fair for light blue flowers; Good for white flowers if dusted with white chalk before pressing—if not dusted, they will dry gray.

Dianthus (Pink) Basic press. Color durability is Poor.

Dracaena Leaf Microwave one leaf at a time in padded pressboard on ¾ power for 30 seconds. Let rest five minutes. Microwave again for 30 seconds. Repeat as needed. Occasionally used in wedding bouquets. Color durability is Poor.

Dusty Miller Leaf Basic press with heat. Dust with chalk before pressing. These leaves can be grown in a variety of shapes and sizes, from fern-like leaves 2″ long to very large, wide leaves 6″ long. Color durability, when chalked, is Best.

Eugenia Leaf Book. Young leaves dry mahogany with Fair durability. Mature leaves age to sepia. Color durability is Poor for natural color.

Felicia Basic press. Color durability is Poor.

Festuca (Fescue Grass) Book. Very nice curves for use as stems or as special effects when colored with felt-pen ink for durability. Color durability is Poor, ages to straw color.

Forget-Me-Not (Myosotis) Basic press, in sprays or individual florets. Difficult to pick the florets and remove calyx from back of each tiny floret, but well worth the effort. Florets shrink easily if not properly supported by very fresh, springy, polyester-padded pressboard and pressure. Color durability is Best.

Freesia Microwave and conventional oven. Remove excess overlapping florets and buds. Brush small amount of chalk on petals and buds only. Microwave one spray in one pressboard on ¾ power for two minutes. Let stand 10 minutes under pressure. Repeat microwaves until petals are dry. Finish drying stem and calyx in oven. Color durability is Fair.

Gardenia
Preparing the Flower

Florists use paraffin wax in the center of gardenias to hold the petals in an upright position. This wax must be carefully removed without tearing the petals. Gently squeeze the hard wax through the petals, breaking it away into small pieces that can be removed with care. Cut the stem off, close to the flower.

Carefully separate the layers of petals (Illus. AG–10). Gardenias are made up of three sets of

Illus. AG-10. Gardenia must be taken apart in order to press them successfully. Divide the three levels of petals and pull out the loosely-connected central petals.

petals, each one smaller in size. Petals at the center of the flower are loosely connected.

Dusting the Flowers with Chalk

Drop the flower parts in a covered bowl of powdered tempera chalk. Shake the bowl to distribute chalk on the petals.

Remove the petals from the chalk, shaking excess chalk from the petals, and then rub remaining chalk into petals.

Pressing Flowers in the Microwave Oven

Lay only *one* set of petals on a plain piece of chipboard, face down. Cover the back of the flower petals with a thin padded pressboard.

Put only *one* sandwich of petals in microwave oven. More than one sandwich will slow the action of the microwaves, and the flowers will discolor. Microwave one minute on ¾ power.

Let flowers stand under pressure for about half an hour.

Check to see if petals are dry. Return each sandwich of flower petals separately to microwave again for 30 seconds, if needed.

Let petals stand again for half an hour. Check to see if the petals are dry. Microwave again at 30 second intervals as necessary.

Note: These flowers must be completely dried in the microwave oven. If they are left to finish drying in the basic press they will discolor. If the microwave timing is increased to dry the flower faster, blisters may appear on the petals.

Gardenias will dry an ivory color and age to uneven grays. The pigments of chalk are not absorbed by the petals to color the flower for durability. Chalk is only used as an aid for drying the flowers.

Painting the Gardenias

Gardenias from wedding bouquets will sometimes be badly discolored when they are re-

ceived. This discoloration cannot be corrected. At other times, the flowers will be received in a limp condition, but still white. Because of these varying conditions, results will be inconsistent from one bouquet to the next. Painting wedding gardenias will keep results consistent from bride to bride. See Chapter 3 for instructions on mixing and applying paint.

Reassembling Gardenias

After the petals have been painted, trim away any ruffled edges or bits of paint that may have adhered to the edges of the petals.

Cut three small loose petals in a kidney shape and intertwine the three (or two) petals together for the center of the flower.

Lay the graduated sequence of petals on top of each other, smallest on top (Illus. AG–11). It is not necessary to tape or glue the flower parts of a gardenia together because the flower can easily be moved by grasping its middle firmly between the tongs of a long tweezers. Color durability is Poor.

Illus. AG-11. To reassemble the flower, lay the three sets of petals down in the proper order. Then, cut the three loose petals into kidney shapes, interlock them, and place them on top of the others.

Geranium, Pelargonium Florets from the large, round cluster of these flowers are very slow to dry. Single florets are better than double. The many layers of petals in double florets add to moisture content, and the flower takes too long to dry, increasing the chance of discoloration. Darker reds dry to a dull red, whereas salmon-colored flowers dry to a bright red. Peach-colored flowers dry a nice pink. Color durability varies. This is a very large family of flowers and each must be tested separately.

Geranium, Cranesbill (Lancastrian, Grandiflorum, Incanum, Sanguineum) Basic press. Color durability is Fair to Poor.

Geranium, Flower Spring Basic press with heat. This plant is used by flower arrangers primarily for its variegated leaves—green with white around outer edges. Flowers are sparse, single, salmon red, with only two to four florets to a cluster. Color durability is Best.

Geranium, Ivy Leaf (Pelargonium Peltatum) Color is sensitive when originally pressed. Watch for water spots. Better success can be had when this flower is partially dried in microwave oven and then completed in the basic press with heat. Use caution because the flower can become fused to the chipboard in a microwave oven. Color durability is Excellent.

Geranium Leaves, Variegated Microwave, to prevent color loss. Durability is Poor.

Geranium, Martha Washington Basic press with heat.

Geranium, Pansy (Madam Layal) Basic press without heat. Color durability is Fair for lavender petals, Best for dark purple petals.

Geranium, Rose Basic press, no heat. Color durability is Best.

Geum (Avens) Basic press. Color durability is Fair.

Gladiolus Basic press. The individual flowers of gladiolus must be removed from the stalk, treated with chalk, pressed, and reassembled. Follow directions for pressing lilies. Besides the flowers, pull the petals from buds, chalk them, and press them separately. Also press the sheaths of these buds if the flower is to be reassembled as a stalk.

Assembling Stalk of Gladiolus

Follow instructions for reassembling lilies. After the individual flowers have been reassembled, they can be arranged in a pressed-flower picture one above the other just as they grew—the smaller flowers at the top of the stalk, buds with sheaths at the very tip, and a wide stem inserted below the column of flowers (Illus. AG–12). (Gladiolus leaves can be split, pressed, and used as wide stems.)

Gladiolus Used in Wedding Bouquets

Stalks of gladiolus are sometimes used in wedding bouquets, but more often, the individual

Illus. AG-12. Gladiolus stalks must be taken apart, the flowers pressed individually, and then the whole reassembled afterward.

Illus. AG-13. Many florists make contrived flowers for wedding bouquets from the petals of gladiolus. They have given this type of flower the name glamellia.

flowers are removed from the stalk and used throughout the bouquet in the same way as lilies.

Glamellia

Florists have created a flower for wedding bouquets that they call a glamellia (Illus. AG–13). It is made up of many petals from the gladiolus, glued one behind the other with rubber cement, creating a many-petalled flower anywhere from 4 to 8 inches across. When preserving such a flower from a wedding bouquet, all the petals must be taken apart with care, chalked, pressed separately, and then reconstructed to the original measurements.

Measure the flowers from the bride's bouquet and make notes about the size and placement of the glamellias. If the petals display an outer edge or inner throat with a blush of color, such as a pink lip on white petals, chalk the petals with white powdered tempera to aid drying and, after they have dried, rub a bit of pink chalk into the lip of the flower, blending it back into the white color for a natural appearance. Color durability: Good for white and light-colored flowers, when chalked. Excellent for brightly colored flowers, when chalked.

Goldenrod Basic press. Color durability is Poor.

Grass Basic press. Prairie grasses with a fountain-like growth habit develop graceful golden stalks of seed that are very effective. Color durability of gold is Best.

Grevillia Basic press. Color durability is Poor.

Heather Basic press. Florets pulled from spray very nice for tiny embellishments. Color durability is Fair, ages to deeper rose color, then to rust red.

Hibiscus Basic press. Color durability is Poor.

Holly Leaf Cannot be pressed with good shape because of the stiff unyielding thorn curving at the end of the leaf.

Hollyhock Basic press. Color durability is Poor.

Hydrangea Basic press. Press florets individu-ally. Color unreliable. Pinks may dry lavender; lavender may dry pink. Shape of florets very nice; smaller florets good for greeting cards and sta-tionery. Color durability is Poor.

Indian Hawthorn (Raphiolepis) Basic press. Color durability is Poor.

Iris, Dutch Basic press with heat. Used in wedding bouquets occasionally.

Preparing the Flowers

Remove petals from the flower. Dust with chalk to match. Blue Dutch iris is closer to the purple color of tempera chalk than it is to the blue. Yellow markings will not show up well through the chalk. Place petals in the basic press and put in oven.

Reconstructing the Flower

Cut one large petal lengthwise and trim base of another large petal as shown in Illus. AG–14.

Illus. AG-14. Prepare iris petals for the press by cut-ting one crosswise and one lengthwise.

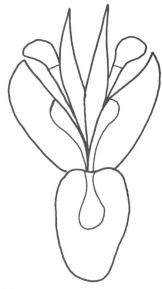

Illus. AG-15. Reconstruct the iris with the cut pieces of petal and the whole, pressed, narrow petals.

Arrange petals as shown (Illus. AG–15). Turn flower upside down and tape petals together with masking tape. Turn flower right side up and insert as many of the long narrow petals as neces-sary to achieve the required effect. Discard re-mainder of the petals.

If it is difficult to turn the flower upside down, arrange the petals on a padded pressboard, cover the flowers with chipboard, and turn the sand-wich upside down. Carefully remove the padded pressboard from the back of the flower and apply tape to the petals. Color durability is Excellent when chalked.

Ivy Leaf Book or basic press with heat. Color durability is Fair. For variegated white and green ivy, see Algerian ivy.

Japanese Maple Leaf Book.

Johnny-jump-up (Viola Tricolor) Basic press. Color durability is Best.

Lantana Basic press. Color durability is Poor.

Larkspur Basic press. Excellent subject for pressed flower crafts. Color durability is Best for white and dark blue, Fair for light blue and deep pink, but Poor for light pink.

Leatherleaf Fern Basic press with heat. Color durability is Poor.

Leptospermum Basic press. Press singles only. Color durability is Fair.

Lilac Microwave. Break large clusters of florets into small pieces on one padded pressboard. Microwave on ¾ power for two minutes. Let stand ten minutes. Repeat microwave until petals are dry.

To reassemble cluster of flowers, arrange several of the small pieces to form clusters. Used in wedding bouquets occasionally. Color durability is Poor.

Lily Book or basic press, except Microwave for rubrum lilies. There are many varieties of lilies and most can be pressed with success when the

flower has been dismantled, and chalk applied.
Preparing the Flower

Remove all the petals and stamens and discard the stem (AG–16). Press stamens in a book.

Drop the petals into a covered bowl of powdered tempera chalk mixed to match the color of the flower. Shake bowl to distribute the chalk on the petals. Remove excess chalk and rub remainder of chalk into the petals.

Illus. AG-16. Take lilies completely apart and discard the stem before pressing.

Pressing the Petals

Lay the petals face up on a thin padded pressboard (or in a book), allowing some of the petals to retain their natural curl and straightening others. Cover the face of the petals with a plain chipboard.

Put the press (or book with brick for weight) in an oven with just the pilot light for heat.
Coloring the Petals

Brightly colored lilies can be colored with felt-pen ink after the petals have dried, and pastel-colored flowers can be colored with powdered tempera chalk rubbed into the petals. If the flower displays a blush of another color, such as a pink lip on a white petal, chalk the flower with white powdered tempera to dry the flower. After the petals have dried, rub a bit of pink chalk into the lip of the flower, blending it back into the white for a natural appearance.

Assembling Lily

Arrange two wide petals so that the spines and base of each radiate towards the center of the flower.

Trim away lower portion of one wide petal as shown in Illus. AG–17, rounding the shape to create perspective.

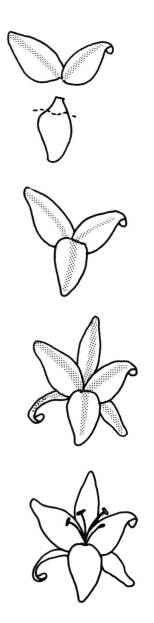

Illus. AG-17. To reconstruct a lily, place two petals together, cut a third petal so that it appears to bend forward, attach the two small petals, and place the stamens between the petals.

Lay the trimmed petal over the base of the other petals, lining up spines to radiate towards the center of the flower.

Slip the remaining three narrow petals under and between the three wide petals. Petals that are curled can be inserted between the straight petals where they best create a nice effect. Use your own judgment for placement. In some cases, all curled petals can be used.

Carefully slip a tweezers under the flower and grasp all parts of the flower between the tweezers' prongs. Turn the flower upside down on the workbench and tape parts together with a small piece of masking tape across the back of the flower.

If you find it difficult to turn the flower over, assemble the flower on a padded pressboard. When the flower is ready to be turned over, cover the face of the flower with a chipboard and turn the sandwich upside down. Carefully remove the padded pressboard covering the back of the flower and apply the tape.

Turn the flower right side up and insert stamens in center of flower, slipping them down between the petals.

Lily, Rubrum   The petals of a rubrum lily are a bright pink in the center and have maroon-colored spots and white edges. It is a very beautiful but difficult flower that is used now and then in wedding bouquets. Follow directions given for preparing, dismantling, and applying chalk to other lilies, but see below for special drying instructions.

Pressing the Flower

Lay only two large or three small petals on each padded pressboard. Straighten some of the petals and allow others to retain their natural curl. If more than three petals are microwaved at one time, the action of the microwaves will be slowed and the petals may discolor. Cover the face of the petals with plain chipboard.

Microwave one sandwich of petals on ¾ power for two minutes.

After the petals have been removed from the microwave, keep them under pressure until thoroughly dry.

The pink color will be very dull after the petals have dried, and dots will be barely visible. If this flower is dried any other way it will discolor. Considering this, the dull pink color is not so bad. Coloring the flower with felt-pen ink is essential if a wedding bouquet is to be reproduced for the best appearance. Felt-pen ink must be used to color the entire petal of the flower. The white edges cannot be saved. When felt-pen ink is applied to the petals, the spots show up more prominently.

Reassemble the flower as directed for other types of lilies.

Lily of the Valley   Microwave and basic press with heat. First, dust with white chalk. Then, microwave three sprays in one padded pressboard on ¾ power for one minute. Finish drying in basic press with heat. Florets will shrivel if dried too fast in the microwave oven. Color durability is Fair.

Lobelia   Basic press. Color durability is Best.

Love-in-a-Mist (Nigella)   Basic press. Color durability is Poor.

Maidenhair Fern   Basic press or book. Dry, shriveled maidenhair fern from wedding bouquets can be revived before pressing. Put fern in a plastic bag with dab of water and seal bag

tightly. Leave in refrigerator for a day. Color durability is Poor for leaves (age to white) but Best for black stems.

Maidenhair Fern, Hawaiian   Microwave and basic press with heat. A very stiff, heavily needled fern that looks like pine. It is used in wedding bouquets fairly often and is difficult to press and arrange because of its heavy, woody texture. Press only the lighter weight tips of these ferns and individual tufts of needles from the heavy branches. Press in padded pressboard in microwave oven for two minutes on ¾ power. Two or three pressboards can be done at one time. Finish drying in basic press with heat. Color durability is Poor.

Marigold, Dwarf French   Book or basic press. Small, lily-shaped petals in the center of these flowers are excellent tiny flowers for detailed embellishments in a picture. Examine flowers before buying plants. The center petals are sometimes very tightly closed lilies. Look for centers with larger, open lilies. Color durability is Best.

Nandin Leaf   Book. In season, these leaves are red. Mature leaves are green. New growth is mahogany. Color durability is Fair for red and mahogany, and Poor for green (ages to sepia).

Narcissus   Basic press. The cup in the center of these flowers, when crisp, can sometimes crack open when pressure is applied. Allow the sandwich of narcissus flowers to stand for a few hours with only a rubber band for pressure. Once the flower has become somewhat limp in the center, it will not crack when pressure is applied. Color durability is Fair for white and Poor for yellow.

Nasturtium   Basic press. Color durability is Poor.

Oleander   Basic press. Color durability is Fair.

Orchid, Cattleya   Borax mattress press. Orchids retain an exceptional amount of moisture and can be pressed with good results several days after they have been picked. However, cattleya orchids from a wedding bouquet, already without water for eight hours or more, should be pressed as soon as possible.

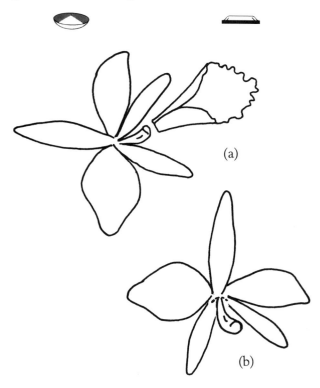

Illus. AG-18. Remove both the throat and the tongue from the cattleya orchid before pressing.

Preparing the Flower

Remove stem from the flower, cutting close to petals with sharp knife. Discard stem.

Break throat off flower (Illus. AG–18a).

Remove tongue, cutting close to petals with a sharp knife (Illus. AG–18b). Discard tongue.

Separate the five remaining petals.

Orchids contain certain chemicals that, when exposed to oxygen during drying, cause the flowers to discolor. Though microwaves prevent this from occurring in the sturdy cymbidium orchids, the delicate petals of cattleya orchids fare better when dipped in Quick Dip liquid silver cleaner and dried in the borax mattress press, as an antioxidant.

Quick Dip™ silver cleaner is sold in the household cleaning section of supermarkets. Please note warning on label: "Harmful if swallowed—irritant. Keep out of reach of children," and "CAUTION: Contains thiorea. Keep away from eyes. Use with adequate ventilation."

Dip only the throat in Quick Dip, using a long tweezers to handle the flower. Cover the bottle of Quick Dip immediately.

Lay throat on paper towelling immediately and pat the throat dry with another length of paper towelling. Handle the throat with tweezers and protect your hands with a paper towel as you blot. Discard the wet paper from time to time and use fresh paper towelling as the work progresses.

Caution: Do not allow Quick Dip to remain on the petals more than a few seconds before you blot and pat dry. Chalk must be applied right after the petal has been blotted. If chalk is not applied immediately, the petals will turn black. If the petals of a colored flower are not quickly blotted and neutralized with the chalk, the color from the flower will bleed. Do not devise production-line methods for treating cattleya petals. Finish chalking each petal before dipping the next in Quick Dip.

Brush powdered tempera chalk mixed to match the color of the flower onto the throat. The application of chalk will neutralize the action of the chemical. Rub the chalk into the petal.

Repeat the same procedure with each of the remaining five petals.

Immediately after you have finished treating the flowers, remove the paper towels saturated with Quick Dip so that the fumes do not permeate the air of your work space.

Pressing the Petals

Open throat out flat and lay it face down on the borax mattress press.

Lay the five petals on the mattress face down.

Cover the backs of the petals with polyester double-knit fabric and lay a thick pad of polyester fibrefill over the double-knit fabric. Place cover on the press and put the press in an oven with only the pilot light for heat.

Add heavy weights (around 35 pounds) on top of the press. Flowers from a wedding bouquet will dry more quickly than freshly picked flowers. The throat and three narrow petals will dry first, the two large petals last.

Check the flowers each day. If the petals are limp or cold to the touch, they are not dry. Check for the beginnings of discoloration. If necessary, brush additional chalk onto the petals and return the press to the warm oven until they are dry.

Reassembling the Flower

Brush excess chalk from throat and all the petals of the flower. Rub remainder of chalk into the petals, or add fresh chalk and rub into petals for sharp color.

If chalk has caked on the petals unevenly and cannot be removed with a brush, apply acetone (fingernail polish remover) to the petal, gently blot with facial tissue to remove chalk, and re-chalk when dry.

Add yellow chalk to center of throat using a cotton-tipped swab and blend edges for a natural appearance.

If lip of the throat is a darker color than the body of the throat, add the second color into the lip, blending edges of the color into the body of the throat.

For perspective and a further appearance of depth, apply chalk in a color slightly darker than the color of the flower into the base of the two large petals, blending color into the body of the

petal. For example, on white cattleyas, use gray chalk.

Profile Throat

Cut throat down the center and, with curved cutting tool, cut a curve on each half as shown in Illus. AG–19.

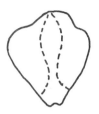

Illus. AG-19. To create a profile view of the orchid throat, cut the throat in two pieces and arrange them one on top of the other.

Arrange one half of the throat on top of the other, allowing the piece in back to protrude slightly.

Slip a tweezers under the two parts and firmly grasp between the prongs. Turn the throat upside down and tape parts together with a small piece of masking tape across the back. Turn throat right side up. With scissors, trim base of the throat to a suitable rounded shape and set aside.

Full-Face Throat

Cut the throat in three pieces as shown in Illus. AG–20. The lip will be triangular in shape.

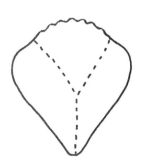
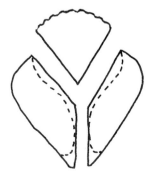

Illus. AG-20. To create a full-face throat, cut the petal in three pieces as shown and cut curves into the two side pieces.

With the curved cutting tool, cut a curve on the edge of each of the two outer parts of the throat, and trim away any discoloration present at the base of these parts.

To reassemble the throat, place the two pieces face up on either side of the triangle-shaped lip, with curved sides along the outer edges.

Illus. AG-21. To reassemble the petal, place the two throat pieces on either side of the triangular lip.

Slip a tweezers under the petal and firmly grasp all parts of the throat. Turn the petal upside down and tape parts together with a small piece of masking tape across the back.

If you find it difficult to turn the throat upside down, arrange the pieces on a padded press-board. When it is ready to turn over, cover with chipboard and turn the sandwich upside down. Remove the padded pressboard and apply tape to the back of the throat. With a scissors, trim bottom of throat to a suitable rounded shape.

Joining Throat to Set of Five Petals
(Illus. AG–22)

Place the two largest petals opposite each other with spines radiating towards the center. Place the throat, profile or full face, on top of the two large petals at the point where they meet.

Insert a long narrow petal on either side of the throat, slipping it under and behind the throat. Insert the third narrow petal below and under the throat. Check the arrangement of petals to make sure the spines of the two large petals and the three long petals radiate towards the center of the flower. All the petals and the throat should appear to be connected at the base of the flower.

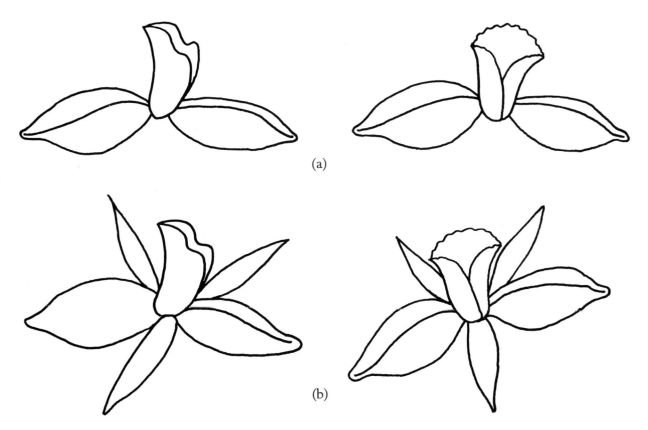

(a)

(b)

Illus. AG-22a & b. Begin reconstructing the flower by joining the two large petals at the tips. Then, for a profile view, place the profile throat on the two petals (a). Insert the rest of the petals underneath the two large petals. For a full-face flower, place the full-face throat on top of the two petals and tuck the other petals underneath the two large petals (b).

Illus. AG-23. Hold all of the pieces together by turning the flower over and placing a small piece of tape over the back of the flower.

Slip a tweezers under the petals and turn the flower upside down on the workbench. Tape the parts together with a small piece of masking tape across the back (Illus. AG–23), making certain all the petals are held by the tape. A second small piece of tape might be needed to hold the lower narrow petal. Color durability is Excellent.

Orchid, Cymbidium   Microwave.
Preparing the Flower (Illus. AG–24)

Remove stem from flower, cutting it off close to the petals with a sharp knife. Break throat off flower.

Split the throat, cutting down through the center with a sharp knife. Remove tongue from the set of five petals, cutting it off close to the petals with a sharp knife. The tongue can be discarded. The remaining set of five petals can be left intact.
Microwaving the Throats

Do not use chalk on throats.

Arrange the two pieces of throat on a piece of plain chipboard and cover them with a generous piece of fluffy fibrefill, followed by a padded pressboard.

Microwave 30 seconds on ¾ power.

Open sandwich and remove the fibrefill. The two halves of the throat should be limp and more

easily handled at this point, so they can be flattened out against the chipboard.

Discard the piece of fibrefill and cover throat with only the padded pressboard. Microwave two minutes on full power.

If the throat is limp and not crisp, it is not dry. Microwave again at 30-second intervals until dry. It is important to dry the throat completely. If left to dry on its own, without the aid of a microwave, it will discolor.

Do not allow for standing time between shots in the microwave oven. The dark maroon, striped markings on cymbidium throats bleed into the white areas when the throats are not dried quickly.

The striped markings on the inside of the throats will show through to the outside surface of the throat after it has dried. I know of no way this can be prevented.

Illus. AG-24. When pressing a cymbidium orchid, remove the throat and tongue (discard this), then split the throat down the center.

Applying Chalk to Petals

Drop the set of five petals in a covered bowl of powdered tempera chalk mixed to match the flower. Shake the bowl to distribute the chalk on the petals. Remove flowers and brush away excess chalk from the petals. Rub remaining chalk into the petals.
Microwaving the Set of Five Petals

Lay the petals face up on a thin padded pressboard and cover the front of the petals with a plain piece of chipboard.

Microwave one minute on ¾ power.

Remove from microwave and let stand 30 minutes while under pressure. If the flowers are limp and cold to the touch, they are not dry.

Return the sandwich of petals to microwave again for 30-second intervals with 10 minutes standing time until they are dry. Do not eliminate the standing times or subject the petals to stronger microwaves than necessary, because the petals may develop blisters.

Do not allow these petals to finish drying in the basic press. Discoloration will result.

Reassembling the Flower

Trim away rough edges along inside edges of the throats and fit the two halves together, dovetailing top and bottom edges together (Illus. AG–25). Turn over and tape pieces together on back if slippage is occurring.

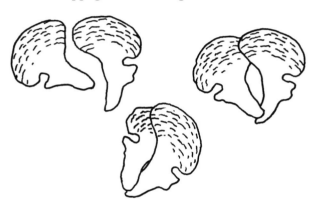

Illus. AG-25. Take the two halves of the throat and dovetail their top and bottom edges.

Lay the throat in the center of the set of five petals. You may dismantle the set of five petals to trim or shorten them if you wish. Color durability is Excellent.

Orchid, Dendrobium

Preparing the Flowers

Remove the flowers from the spray, pinching stems off close to the flower.

Remove buds, leaving length of stem attached. Split buds and stems in half (Illus. AG–26) to reduce moisture and bulk. Do not use chalk on buds.

Illus. AG-26. Split all of the buds and stems of dendrobium orchids before pressing them to reduce bulk.

Break the throat off the sets of five petals.

Cut away the thick growth in the center of the set of five petals, being careful not to cut all the way through the petal.

Applying Chalk to the Flowers

Drop throats and five-petal sets in a covered bowl of chalk mixed to match the color of the flower. Shake the bowl to distribute the chalk on the petals of the flowers. Remove the petals from the bowl and brush away excess chalk clinging to them.

Pressing Throats in Basic Press

Scatter throats on a chipboard sheet and cover with a thick padded pressboard. Apply very minimal pressure, using just two rubber bands to hold the sandwich together. The throats of these flowers can be very crisp and difficult to flatten. After they have been in the pressboard for four hours or so, open the sandwiches and lay the limp throats, now more easily controlled, face down on a plain chipboard sheet and cover with a thin padded pressboard.

Put the sandwiches in the basic press and dry in the oven with only the pilot light for heat.

Microwaving the Set of Five Petals

Lay three sets of petals face up on a thin padded pressboard and cover with a plain chipboard.

Microwave one sandwich of petals on carousel for two minutes on ¾ power.

Let flowers stand under pressure for 30 minutes.

If the flowers feel limp or cold to the touch,

they are not dry. Microwave again for one minute or longer, as necessary, to dry the flower.

After the flowers have dried, keep the sandwiches of flowers under pressure for 24 hours.

Microwaving Buds

Lay three or four of the buds, cut side down, on a thin padded pressboard. Do not apply chalk to buds. Cover with a plain chipboard.

Microwave one sandwich of buds on ¾ power for two minutes.

Let buds stand under pressure for 30 minutes.

Microwave again if necessary.

Reassembling the Flowers

Trim uneven lower edge of the throat to a nice rounded shape and place throat over center of the set of five petals (Illus. AG–27).

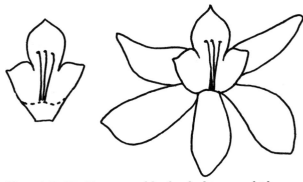

Illus. AG-27. To reassemble dendrobium orchids, cut the throat so that it rests on top of the set of five petals in a natural way.

Slip a tweezers under the flower and firmly grasp the two parts of the flower between the prongs of the tweezers. Turn the flower upside down and tape the two flower parts together with a small piece of masking tape.

Arrange the flowers in a cascading column in a good representation of the spray of flowers as it grows, with several buds inserted at the end of the spray.

Color durability is Excellent.

Orchid, Phalaenopsis Of all the flowers used in wedding bouquets, phalaenopsis orchids are the easiest to press. Even when received in a

limp, droopy condition, they absorb chalk well, drying without discoloration or scarring.

Preparing the Flower

Cut or pinch off stem close to the base of the flower.

Drop the flower into a covered bowl of powdered tempera chalk mixed to match the color of the flower. Shake the bowl to distribute chalk on the petals of the flower. Remove flower from the bowl and rub chalk generously into the petals of the flower.

Pressing the Flowers

Lay a thick blanket of polyester fibrefill on top of the borax mattress.

Lay the flower upside down on top of the fluffy polyester fibrefill. Reach under the flower and spread open the two wings that are in the center of the flower. These wings will be very crisp and cannot be spread open easily at this time.

Cover the back of the flower with a second fluffy blanket of polyester fibrefill and put the cover of the press on top. Put the press in the oven with only the pilot for heat, and put a five pound weight on the press.

Open the press every day and, when the wings in the center of the flower are limp and more easily controlled, you can open and straighten them.

Around the third day, before the flower has dried, open the press and remove the flower from the polyester fibrefill blankets.

Lay the flower face down on the borax mattress pad, opening and straightening the wings again, and cover the back of the flower with the polyester double-knit fabric.

Cover double-knit fabric with the polyester fibrefill blanket and put the cover back on the press.

Put the press back in the oven with a 30-pound weight on top of the press.

Check the flower every day. If the flower is limp and cold to the touch, it is not dry. If the flower is not dry by the fourth day, brush more chalk on the flower before returning it to the oven. Phalaenopsis orchids from a bridal bouquet dry much faster than those that have been freshly picked.

Color durability is Excellent.

Pansy Basic press. Most nurseries feature pansies with very large flowers. For pressed flower crafts, look for plants with smaller flowers in more varied and interesting colors and patterns. Color durability is Fair.

Pearblossom (Evergreen Pear) Basic press. Color durability is Fair.

Periwinkle (Vinca) Basic press. Color durability is Poor.

Petunia Basic press. Color durability is Poor.

Philodendron, Split-Leaf Leaf Sheath Book. Very large tropical plant whose leaves are encased in a sheath similar to the rubber tree. The leaf sheath is 8″ to 12″ long and can be easily pressed with good results. It resembles a tree trunk after it is pressed, making it effective for landscapes. Color durability is Best.

Phlox Basic press. Color durability is Fair for light colors; Good for darker colors.

Pine Book. Some age to red, others to yellow.

Poinsettia Basic press with heat. Remove thick stamens from center of flower and discard. Dust flower with matching chalk and press in basic press with heat. Color durability is Excellent.

Pomegranate Flowers Basic press. Cut away thick growth under flower where fruit will develop. Loose petals can be pressed with greater ease and used to form a contrived flower. Color durability is Best.

Pothos Leaves Microwave, ½ power, two leaves in one sandwich for two minutes. Let stand five minutes. Microwave again as needed with five-minutes standing time between shots. (¾ power can blister or scorch these leaves.) Occasionally used in wedding bouquets. Color durability is Poor.

Prayer Plant (Maranta) Microwave. One leaf in one sandwich for two minutes on ¾ power. Occasionally used in wedding bouquets. Color durability is Poor.

Primrose (English and Malacoides) Basic press. Color durability is Poor.

Queen Anne's Lace Basic press. Remove florets and press separately. Press some of the florets full face, others in profile with stems attached. Press remaining skeleton of stems as well.

To reassemble the flower head, arrange a cluster using full-face florets in center surrounded by profiles for perspective.

For profile of flower head, use skeleton of stems in profile. Arrange profile florets at ends of stems; full-face florets closer to base of the network of stems. Color durability is Best.

Rabbit's-Foot Fern   Book. Color durability is Poor.

Roses, Small to Miniature   Basic press with heat. Miniature roses that open flat when full blown, such as Carousel, Cricket, and Holy Toledo, can be pressed with good results.

Pressing the Rose in Profile

For upright miniature roses and small commercially grown roses such as Sweethearts, split the rose in two. Follow instructions for splitting roses found in Chapter 4.

Carefully scrape the stamens out of the back of the cut rose to reduce moisture content. Set rose aside.

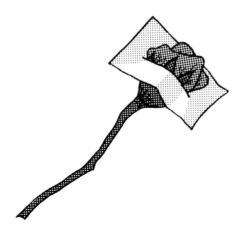

Illus. AG-28. A piece of paper with a slit in its middle will enable you to arrange and hold rose petals while pressing.

Cut slit about ¾″ to 1″ long in a small piece of paper for a support that will control the petals on either side of the rose.

Pull the stem of the rose down through the slit in the paper until the calyx and petals of the rose are caught between the slit in the paper (Illus. AG-28). Fold side petals on either end of the rose in a natural and pleasing arrangement so that the cut ends of the petals are turned under. The paper form will hold the petals in place.

Lay the rose, in its paper support, upside down on a plain chipboard sheet. Cover cut side of rose with an appropriate size padded pressboard. If a curved stem is desirable and the stem is rigid and stiff, use masking tape to hold the stem in position. Put press in oven with only pilot light for heat. Color durability: Best for pink sweetheart roses; Fair for Carousel, Holy Toledo, Cricket, and Born Free.

Rose, Tea   Full-size tea roses, with petals closed in an upright position, are difficult to press with good color and good shape. The many layers of moist petals pressing against each other causes discoloration. There are two aspects of color to consider when pressing rose petals—the inside surface of the petal and the outside surface. It is the outside surface that we see when a rose is pressed in profile, yet the best natural color on a rose petal is found on the inside surface. The inside surface of a rose petal also absorbs pigments from the chalk more efficiently, further enhancing and fixing the natural color of the petal. From this, you can see why roses are difficult to press whole with good color.

On the following pages, instructions are given for drying rose petals with an application of chalk as an aid to drying the petals. An exception is the red rose. Applying red chalk does not improve the color of red rose petals. The petals will dry a maroon or burgundy color and the bright red chalk will be in obvious contrast to the dark color of the petal. Red rose petals should be dried without an application of chalk.

Preparing the Petals

Discard petals that are damaged or discolored. Remove six to eight petals that are in good condition. Set remainder of rose aside. If the petals are severely cupped, snip off the bottom tip of the petals (Illus. AG–29) to release fullness and/or make a small cut into the bottom of the petals.

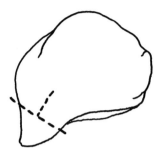

Illus. AG-29. Rose petals will not press flat unless you first remove their bases and cut a small slit in their lower ends.

Drop the petals into a covered bowl of powdered tempera chalk mixed to match the color of the petals. Shake the bowl to distribute the chalk on the petals. Open the bowl and remove the petals, using a long tweezers, onto a piece of facial tissue. Shake excess chalk from the petals as you remove them from the bowl. Rub the remaining chalk into the petals.

Pressing Petals

Lay the petals close together, but not overlapping, on the borax mattress.

Cover the petals with polyester double-knit fabric.

Lay a blanket of fluffy polyester fibrefill over the double-knit fabric.

Cover the press and put it in an oven with just the pilot for heat.

Lay bricks (20 to 30 pounds) on top of the press. The petals will dry in about 24 hours. Remove from oven and keep petals under pressure a few days after they have dried.

Rose petals can be pressed successfully between the pages of a book which is subjected to heat, but do not press rose petals in padded pressboards. The petals develop ruffled edges.

Preparing the Calyx

With a razor or sharp knife, split the calyx with its remainder of petals still attached. Follow instructions for splitting roses found under "How to Use the Padded Pressboards and Basic Press" on page 37.

Pressing the Calyx

Cut a slit in a two-inch square of paper and slip the stem of the flower down through the slit until the calyx is caught between the paper, holding sepals in an upright position.

Or if you prefer to press the sepals down, fold the sepals downwards about ⅛ of an inch above the base of the sepals. (When reassembling the rose, petals are wedged between the sepals and the body of the rose.)

If sepals are difficult to control, wait a few hours. When they are limp, they can be more easily managed.

In many wedding bouquets, rose calyxes will have no stems attached. For this, a 5″ × 8″ sheet of paper can be cut with six slits, so that six calyxes can be pressed at one time.

Lay the rose calyx, in its paper support, face up on a padded pressboard. Cover face of the calyx with a plain chipboard sheet. Press in basic press without heat. Heat will cause the calyxes to dry before they have flattened properly. Heat can be applied after the fifth day to accelerate drying.

Reassembling Rose in Calyx—Sepals Down

Remove excess chalk from petals. Trim the bottom of a large petal in a serpentine curve, as shown in Illus. AG–30, cutting away the lower half of the petal. Turn top edge of the petal down on two sides and pinch to form two cuffs at the top of the petal. (When humidity is low, petals tend to crack as they are folded. In this case, introduce moisture with a humidifier or wet cloth under the petals, or blow on the petal as you might do to fog your glasses.)

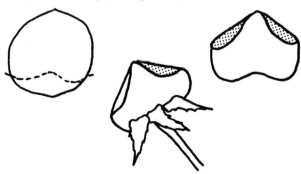

Illus. AG-30. To reassemble a rose with sepals down, cut a petal in a curve and make two folds in the top part as shown.

Insert this petal under the folded sepals of the rose. The calyx with sepals down should have been pressed so that there is space to wedge the petal between the sepals and the body of the rose.

For this section, see Illus. AG–31–33. Fold top edge of two medium-size petals and pinch to form a cuff on one side of each petal. Insert these petals behind the other petal (Illus. AG–31).

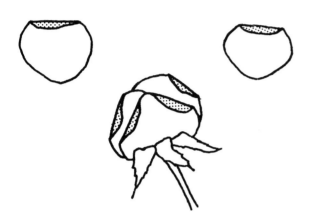

(b)

With curved cutting tool, trim top of two or three petals with an inverted curve as shown. Insert these petals behind the others to complete the rose (Illus. AG–33).

Illus. AG-31. Make folds in two more petals and insert these behind the first.

Illus. AG-33. To complete the rose with sepals down, trim the bases of two or three petals and tuck them behind the folded petal.

Roses with sepals down are best to use for the flowers in the middle of a wedding bouquet, or when a single rose is to be displayed in a frame.
Reassembling Rose in Calyx—Sepals Up

Remove excess chalk from petals. Cut one petal in half. With curved cutting tool, trim edge of each half petal as shown in Illus. AG–34.

Fold a small petal in half. Turn the front edge of the petal back to form a cuff on the front edge of the folded petal (Illus. AG–32a), and insert this petal behind the other petals so it protrudes slightly above the others (Illus. AG–32b).

(a)

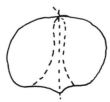

Illus. AG-32a & b. Fold a petal in half and make a second small fold in the top half (a). Then place the folded petal behind the three other petals (b).

Illus. AG-34. Begin reconstructing the sepals-up rose by cutting one petal in two kidney-shaped pieces.

Turn small edge of petal down and pinch to form a cuff on each of the half petals, as shown in Illus. AG–35a. Insert the two halves, one on each side, under the sepals of the calyx. Insert a second set of these petal halves behind the first (Illus. AG–35b).

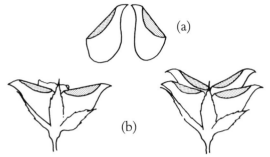

Illus. AG-35a & b. Make folds in the top outer edges of the two petal pieces (a). Place them at either side of the calyx. Repeat the process with a second set of petals (b).

Fold a small petal in half. Turn a small edge of the petal back and pinch to form a cuff on the front edge of the folded petal. Insert this petal behind the others (Illus. AG–36).

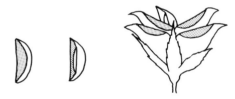

Illus. AG-36. Fold a small petal in half and make a fold in the front half. Place it behind the four folded petals.

With curved cutting tool, trim two to three full-size petals with an inverted curve at the top of the petals and insert these behind the other petals to complete the rose (Illus. AG–37).

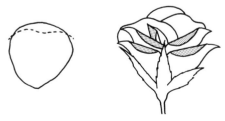

Illus. AG-37. Complete the flower by cutting curves in the tops of two or three petals and placing them behind the others.

Reassembling Rose Bud (Illus. AG–38)

Remove excess chalk from petals. Fold a large petal in half and turn a small edge of the petal back. Pinch to form a cuff on the front edge of the folded petal.

Insert folded petal into a calyx that has only two sepals very close together. Do not allow the base of the folded petal to protrude beyond the sepals. Trim as needed.

Insert a second petal, folded in the same manner, inside the first. Trim width at the base of the second petal as needed.

Illus. AG-38. Reconstruct buds by folding in half two petals and making small folds in their fronts. Then, tuck them into a pressed rose-bud calyx.

Durability of color: Some red roses are more durable than others. Wild red roses lose their natural coloring within a year and turn rust red, whereas commercially grown red roses retain their color for 5 to 7 years. The natural color of white, yellow, and pink roses will age to beige in one or two years. Roses treated with chalk will be appreciably more durable. The darker the pink or yellow chalk used, the more durable the color will be. When white chalk has been used on white rose petals, the color alters only slightly after eight years.

Rubber Tree Leaf Sheaths Book. These are very effective when used for a driftwood effect among the flowers. Remove sheath after the leaf has opened. Allow leaf sheaths to lie on the workbench several hours until they shrivel a bit. Then press in a book. Split wide sheaths in half lengthwise for a better assortment of sizes. Color durability is Best.

Sage   Basic press. Color durability is Fair.

Salvia   Basic press. Color durability is Poor.

Silk Oak Leaves   Book. Color durability is Poor (ages to grey).

Sparaxis   Microwave, one spray in one sandwich on ¾ power for two minutes. Let stand 10 minutes under pressure. Repeat microwave until petals dry. Finish drying stems and calyx in basic press with heat.

Spider Plant Leaves   Microwave one leaf in one padded pressboard on ¾ power for two minutes. Let stand 10 minutes under pressure. Repeat until dry. Very touchy. Can sometimes discolor—even in the microwave. These leaves are sometimes used in wedding bouquets and must be dried with good color. If discoloration persists, try chalk or split wide leaves lengthwise—this helps reduce the bulk in thick center of the leaf and it dries with better color. Color durability is Poor.

Spirea   Basic press. Use singles only. Doubles have poor shape. Both buds and flowers are nice for miniature arrangements. Color durability is Fair.

Statice   Basic press. Color durability is Best.

Stephanotis   Microwave and basic press.

Preparing the Flower for Full-Face View

The flower can be pressed full face with the shank folded under the flower head, or the flower can be cut off the shank about ¼" below the flower. If the flower is cut closer than ¼", it could dry with a hole in the middle. Discard shank.

Preparing Flower for ¾ View

Cut flower from shank (Illus. AG–39a), leaving ¼" stump of the shank on the flower, but do not discard severed shank.

Split shank lengthwise (Illus. AG–39b) and discard one half.

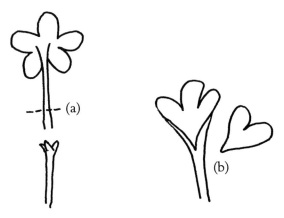

Illus. AG-39. To prepare stephanotis, cut the flower away from its shank and split the shank lengthwise.

Preparing the Flower for Profile View

Pull calyx off shank of the flower, if it is present. Fold sepals of the calyx upwards and press in a book.

Cut off the hard growth at the base of the tubular shank (Illus. AG–40a).

Cut or tear two petals from the flower (Illus. AG–40b).

Illus. AG-40a & b. For a profile view, remove the base of the shank (a). Then, remove two petals from the flower.

Applying Chalk to the Flower Parts

Drop parts of the flowers (but not the calyx) in a covered bowl of white chalk. Shake bowl to distribute the chalk on the flowers. Using a long tweezers, remove flower parts from the chalk and shake excess chalk from the pieces.

Drop the flower parts on a piece of facial tissue. Rub remaining chalk into the petals.

Microwaving the Flowers

Lay no more than three flowers or the parts from three flowers face up on a thin padded pressboard. Cover the face of the flowers with a plain chipboard.

Put only one sandwich of flowers in the microwave oven at one time on ¾ power for one minute. Stephanotis will not be completely dry in one minute. If these flowers are totally dried in the microwave oven, they can become brittle and/or develop ruffled edges. Flowers that are exceptionally fresh might require 1½ minutes in the microwave oven.

Finish drying in the basic press without heat. These flowers do not like heat. Do not remove the flowers from the press until they are thoroughly dry.

Reassembling Stephanotis

Profile: Arrange a set of two petals in back of a set of three petals, slightly protruding beyond the front petals. Turn the flower upside down and affix with masking tape to hold the flower parts together (Illus. AG–41).

Illus. AG-37. Attach the two petals that you removed to the back of the flower with a small piece of tape.

Three-quarter view: Cut away two petals from the full-face flower (Illus. AG–42b), leaving a curved shape at the top of the flower, or trim petals from the full-face flower, leaving a serpentine shape at the top of the flower as shown. Tape shank to the back of the flower with masking tape to hold the parts of the flower together. Though the flower could be dried with shank attached and folded under the head of the flower, it would result in a very short stem. When shanks are dried separately and taped to the back of the flower, the length of the stem can be adjusted.

Illus. AG-42. To create a three-quarter view, remove two petals from the face of the flower leaving a curved edge at the top of the flower.

The Calyx

Trim blunt lower end of stem/shank of profiles or ¾ flowers and insert shank between sepals of the calyx.

Pressing Stephanotis from Wedding Bouquets

Stephanotis are used extensively in wedding bouquets. It is unlikely you will be called upon to press this flower under any circumstances. When received in good condition, it dries an ivory white and ages to toast. In poor condition it dries a light toast color. If bright a white flower is desirable, follow instructions for painting the flowers found in Chapter 3.

Colored Stephanotis

Florists sometimes spray pink, yellow, blue, or lavender paint onto white stephanotis. The paint is often unevenly applied and the color of the dried flower inconsistent. Paint, mixed to match the color used by the florist, can be applied after the flowers have dried. See instructions for painting flowers found in Chapter 3.

Limp Stephanotis

When the flowers are limp but not dry, they can be revived to a more workable condition with a quick dunking in rubbing alcohol. Be quick. If stephanotis are left in alcohol too long they become brittle, so work fast. Dip quickly, dry each flower on facial tissue immediately afterward, and apply chalk. To prevent brittleness, subject these flowers to microwaves for only half a minute.

Dry Stephanotis

When stephanotis are received in a shriveled, dried condition and already discoloring, they can be revived to a more supple condition in the refrigerator. Put the flowers in a plastic bag with a very small amount of water. If too much water is added, mould will develop on the flowers. Blow air into the bag so that the flowers do not become crushed against each other, fasten the bag shut with a wire tie-wrap, and put the bag of flowers in the refrigerator for about 8 hours.

Note: this method of reviving flowers can only be used on stephanotis, baby's breath, fern, or leaves.

After removing the flowers from the refrigerator, they will be more pliable and can be coaxed and straightened into an acceptable shape.

After the flowers have been revived, apply chalk, lay the flowers and/or flower parts face up on a thin padded pressboard so that they are close together but not touching, and cover face of the flowers with a plain chipboard.

Do not subject these flowers to microwaves or heat.

Put the sandwiches of flowers in the refrigerator to dry with a weight on top of each stack of three sandwiches. These flowers will not dry as white as flowers that were received in good condition.

Stock Basic press with heat. Singles best subject for pressing. Remove excess overlapping buds and florets from back of cluster of flowers to reduce bulk. Dust with chalk to match and then press. Color durability is Excellent when dusted with chalk, Good for white, and Poor for natural color.

Succulent Flowers Not always good subject for pressing. Most age to rust color.

Sweet Pea Microwave. Remove excess florets from back of cluster of flowers. Remove pea from center of each floret to reduce bulk. Dust flowers with chalk mixed to match color of the flower. Arrange one spray on thin padded pressboard. Microwave two minutes on ¾ power. Color durability is Poor.

Tulip Microwave. Cut stem close to flower. Divide flower in two parts, splitting flower down between petals. Discard stamens and pistil. Dust petals with chalk mixed to match color of the flower. Lay two flower parts on thin padded pressboard. Microwave one sandwich at a time on ¾ power for two minutes.

To reassemble, cut U-shape curve at base of one set of petals and slip second set of petals under the first, slightly above the front petals for perspective. Turn flower over and tape petals together with a small piece of masking tape. With curved cutting tool trim edges with a graceful curve on both sides. If stem is desired, select wide stem to simulate thick appearance of a tulip stem. Color durability is uncertain.

Verbena   Basic press. Color durability is Best.

Viola   Basic press. Color durability is Poor.

Wild Radish   Basic press. Color durability is Best for dark purple.

Zinnia   Basic press with heat for larger flowers. Dust with chalk to accelerate drying. Color durability is Fair for darker colors.

Metric Equivalents

INCHES TO MILLIMETRES AND CENTIMETRES

MM—millimetres   *CM—centimetres*

Inches	MM	CM	Inches	CM	Inches	CM
⅛	3	0.3	9	22.9	30	76.2
¼	6	0.6	10	25.4	31	78.7
⅜	10	1.0	11	27.9	32	81.3
½	13	1.3	12	30.5	33	83.8
⅝	16	1.6	13	33.0	34	86.4
¾	19	1.9	14	35.6	35	88.9
⅞	22	2.2	15	38.1	36	91.4
1	25	2.5	16	40.6	37	94.0
1¼	32	3.2	17	43.2	38	96.5
1½	38	3.8	18	45.7	39	99.1
1¾	44	4.4	19	48.3	40	101.6
2	51	5.1	20	50.8	41	104.1
2½	64	6.4	21	53.3	42	106.7
2	76	7.6	22	55.9	43	109.2
3½	89	8.9	23	58.4	44	111.8
4	102	10.2	24	61.0	45	114.3
4½	114	11.4	25	63.5	46	116.8
5	127	12.7	26	66.0	47	119.4
6	152	15.2	27	68.6	48	121.9
7	178	17.8	28	71.1	49	124.5
8	203	20.3	29	73.7	50	127.0

INDEX

The "Alphabetic Guide" is not included in the index.